Current
CONTROVERSIES

Politics and Religion

Other Books in the Current Controversies Series

Politics and Religion

Debra A. Miller, Book Editor

GREENHAVEN PRESS
A part of Gale, Cengage Learning

Detroit • New York • San Francisco • New Haven, Conn • Waterville, Maine • London

Elizabeth Des Chenes, *Director, Publishing Solutions*

© 2013 Greenhaven Press, a part of Gale, Cengage Learning

Gale and Greenhaven Press are registered trademarks used herein under license.

For more information, contact:
Greenhaven Press
27500 Drake Rd.
Farmington Hills, MI 48331-3535
Or you can visit our Internet site at gale.cengage.com

For product information and technology assistance, contact us at

Gale Customer Support, 1-800-877-4253
For permission to use material from this text or product, submit all requests online at
www.cengage.com/permissions

Further permissions questions can be emailed to permissionrequest@cengage.com

Articles in Greenhaven Press anthologies are often edited for length to meet page requirements. In addition, original titles of these works are changed to clearly present the main thesis and to explicitly indicate the author's opinion. Every effort is made to ensure that Greenhaven Press accurately reflects the original intent of the authors. Every effort has been made to trace the owners of copyrighted material.

Cover image © Frederick Bass/fStop/Alamy.

LIBRARY OF CONGRESS CATALOGING-IN-PUBLICATION DATA

Politics and religion / Debra A. Miller, book editor.
    pages cm. -- (Current controversies)
    Includes bibliographical references and index.
    ISBN 978-0-7377-6884-8 -- ISBN 978-0-7377-6885-5 (pbk.)
    1. Religion and politics. I. Miller, Debra A., editor of compilation.
    BL65.P7P6377 2013
    322'.1--dc23

                                              2012051657

Printed in the United States of America
1 2 3 4 5 6 7 16 15 14 13 12

Contents

Chapter 1: Should Religion Play a Role in US Politics?

Yes: Religion Should Play a Role in US Politics

No: Religion Should Not Play a Role in US Politics

Christian evangelicals have changed conservatism into a religious movement over the last several decades. The United States used to have a liberal democracy that featured negotiation with respect for minority views, but the new religion-based conservatism asserts beliefs that cannot be compromised and are not susceptible to logical arguments.

Chapter 2: Does Government Interfere with Religious Freedom?

The Barack Obama administration's action to require religious employers to provide health insurance coverage for government-approved contraceptive methods, sterilization procedures, and related education and counseling is a serious erosion of religious freedoms, especially for Catholics who oppose contraception and their religiously affiliated medical institutions. The government should exempt religious institutions from this requirement.

Chapter 3: What Role Does Religion Play in International Politics?

Election of Islamic political parties in Middle East nations such as Morocco, Tunisia, and Egypt following political uprisings there indicate that the Arab Spring has led to a rise of political Islam. Egypt will be a good test case for what role Islam will play in government and whether a fundamentalist or liberal form of Islam will prevail.

US policymakers have historically associated secular government with democracy and good government and Islamist governments with bad governance. However, this view often empowered dictators, and after the political uprising in Egypt that overthrew an autocratic government, it is time to give real democracy a chance in Muslim-majority countries.

Chapter 4: How Should the United States Balance Religion and Politics in the Future?

Foreword

By definition, controversies are "discussions of questions in which opposing opinions clash" (*Webster's Twentieth Century Dictionary Unabridged*). Few would deny that controversies are a pervasive part of the human condition and exist on virtually every level of human enterprise. Controversies transpire between individuals and among groups, within nations and between nations. Controversies supply the grist necessary for progress by providing challenges and challengers to the status quo. They also create atmospheres where strife and warfare can flourish. A world without controversies would be a peaceful world; but it also would be, by and large, static and prosaic.

The Series' Purpose

The purpose of the Current Controversies series is to explore many of the social, political, and economic controversies dominating the national and international scenes today. Titles selected for inclusion in the series are highly focused and specific. For example, from the larger category of criminal justice, Current Controversies deals with specific topics such as police brutality, gun control, white collar crime, and others. The debates in Current Controversies also are presented in a useful, timeless fashion. Articles and book excerpts included in each title are selected if they contribute valuable, long-range ideas to the overall debate. And wherever possible, current information is enhanced with historical documents and other relevant materials. Thus, while individual titles are current in focus, every effort is made to ensure that they will not become quickly outdated. Books in the Current Controversies series will remain important resources for librarians, teachers, and students for many years.

In addition to keeping the titles focused and specific, great care is taken in the editorial format of each book in the series. Book introductions and chapter prefaces are offered to provide background material for readers. Chapters are organized around several key questions that are answered with diverse opinions representing all points on the political spectrum. Materials in each chapter include opinions in which authors clearly disagree as well as alternative opinions in which authors may agree on a broader issue but disagree on the possible solutions. In this way, the content of each volume in Current Controversies mirrors the mosaic of opinions encountered in society. Readers will quickly realize that there are many viable answers to these complex issues. By questioning each author's conclusions, students and casual readers can begin to develop the critical thinking skills so important to evaluating opinionated material.

Current Controversies is also ideal for controlled research. Each anthology in the series is composed of primary sources taken from a wide gamut of informational categories including periodicals, newspapers, books, US and foreign government documents, and the publications of private and public organizations. Readers will find factual support for reports, debates, and research papers covering all areas of important issues. In addition, an annotated table of contents, an index, a book and periodical bibliography, and a list of organizations to contact are included in each book to expedite further research.

Perhaps more than ever before in history, people are confronted with diverse and contradictory information. During the Persian Gulf War, for example, the public was not only treated to minute-to-minute coverage of the war, it was also inundated with critiques of the coverage and countless analyses of the factors motivating US involvement. Being able to sort through the plethora of opinions accompanying today's major issues, and to draw one's own conclusions, can be a complicated and frustrating struggle. It is the editors' hope that Current Controversies will help readers with this struggle.

Introduction

> "Although the phrase 'separation of church and state' does not appear in the US Constitution, it is widely used and accepted as a constitutional principle."

The United States is known around the world as a secular democracy that embraces the principle of separation of church and state. Unlike the constitutions of many other countries, the US Constitution makes no references to a deity or to a specific religion. Instead, the First Amendment to the Constitution contains the establishment clause, which states that "Congress shall make no law respecting an establishment of religion, or prohibiting the free exercise thereof." This clause simultaneously guarantees both separation of religion from government and the freedom citizens have regarding their religious practice. Yet some US public buildings are decorated with references to God; US currency includes the statement, "In God We Trust"; and US presidents and members of Congress are sworn in by placing their right hand on the Bible or another religious text of their choosing, such as the Koran. The separation of church and state persists, despite the fact that, historically, the majority of Americans have been Christian, and many interpret the work of the Founding Fathers as based on Christian values. In the early 2000s, many US Christians are pushing to expand the role of religion in US policies, politics, and public life, while others assert that government is secular and restrained by law from acting on or affecting religions and religious practice.

The unity of church and state existed in Europe for centuries; governments of many countries were linked with or functioned as one with a national church—an arrangement that prompted religious intolerance and fueled religious wars.

Henry VIII in England, for example, established himself in the early 1500s as the head of the Church of England (also called the Anglican Church), and in reaction to the controlling dictates of the Anglican Church nonconformist minority groups of protestants, among them Puritans, ultimately sought religious freedom by emigrating to North America. These individuals espoused the importance of religious freedom as a separate right over which government ought not to have any power. In the early 1600s, such protesting groups settled many places in modern-day Massachusetts. These included Congregationalists, Calvinistic Presbyterians, Quakers, and other independent sects, and it was members of these diverse Christian but mostly non-Catholic sects who established the thirteen original North American colonies.

Despite their affirmation of freedom of religion, however, many early colonists were intolerant toward other religions. The Puritans, for example, wanted to practice their own religion freely but did not approve of others doing the same, whom they called heathens. In colonial Massachusetts, Puritan zealotry led to the infamous Salem witch trials in 1692 and 1693, in which over fifty people were charged with witchcraft and nearly nineteen were executed. In Virginia, one of the most populated colonies, even the oppressive Church of England found a foothold, sending Anglican missionaries and clergy, who collected taxes from parishioners to run local governments and pay for roads and relief for the poor. In fact, nine of the original thirteen colonies established a state religion, giving churches a great deal of power over political affairs in colonial North America.

By the time of the American Revolution (1775–1783) and the writing of the US Constitution (signed in 1787), many were concerned about the role religion would play in the new nation. Shapers of the Constitution wanted to avoid the religious turmoil and wars that had afflicted European countries for so many centuries. Thomas Jefferson, in particular, felt strongly that there should be no established state religion in the new nation, and he began an effort to guarantee freedom *of* religion as well as freedom *from* religion in his home state of Virginia. In 1777, Jefferson drafted a law—An Act for Establishing Religious Freedom—which was introduced into the Virginia legislature once he became governor in 1779. Although Jefferson's bill was opposed by the Anglican Church, it drew support from other religious groups such as the Baptists, Presbyterians, and Jews who wanted protection from religious persecution. With the help of James Madison, the religious freedom bill passed in the state legislature in 1786, the year before the US Constitution was adopted by the Constitutional Convention in Philadelphia in 1787.

In 1789, the founding fathers, including Jefferson, wrote the first ten amendments to the new Constitution, which came to be known as the Bill of Rights. The First Amendment contained the freedom of religion and establishment of religion clause: "Congress shall make no law respecting an establishment of religion, or prohibiting the free exercise thereof. . . ." Jefferson's Virginia law served as a model for this constitutional protection. The Bill of Rights was adopted by the House of Representatives on August 21, 1789, and went into effect on December 15, 1791, after a process of ratification by three-fourths of the states. Much later, the Fourteenth Amendment was added to the US Constitution, making all the protections of the First Amendment applicable at the state level. As a result, neither the federal government nor the states' governments can establish a national or state religion, and freedom of religion is a right guaranteed for all Americans.

Jefferson was proud of his role in bringing freedom of religion to Virginia and the nation. In 1802, when he was president of the United States, Jefferson wrote a letter to the Danbury Baptist Association of Connecticut, explaining the meaning of the First Amendment's clause prohibiting a government establishment of religion. This letter contains the first known reference to the often repeated phrase "separation of church and state." Jefferson's letter stated, in part:

> I contemplate with solemn reverence that act of the whole American people which declared that their legislature should make no law respecting an establishment of religion, or pro-hibiting the free exercise thereof, thus building a wall of separation between church and state. . . .[1]

James Madison, too, wrote about the need for separation be-tween religion and government. The US Supreme Court sub-sequently interpreted the First Amendment to require a wall of separation between church and state, just as Jefferson and Madison said, so that government is prohibited from adopting any particular religion as an official religion, and it must avoid excessive involvement in religion.

Although the phrase "separation of church and state" does not appear in the US Constitution, it is widely used and ac-cepted as a constitutional principle. Nevertheless, the degree to which religion should be separated from government con-tinues to be debated. The authors of the viewpoints in *Current Controversies: Politics and Religion* offer different views about issues such as whether religion should play a role in US poli-tics, whether government is interfering too much with free-dom of religion, whether religion is having an undue influ-ence on international politics, and how the United States should balance religion and politics in the future.

Notes

1. Select works of Thomas Jefferson, Constitutional Society, www.constitution.org/tj/sep_church_state.htm.

CHAPTER 1

Should Religion Play a Role in US Politics?

Chapter Preface

Since the 1970s, conservative Christian political groups, including Christian Evangelicals, conservative Catholics, and Mormons, have influenced US politics. Christian conservatives, often simply called Evangelicals because of the large numbers of Evangelical/fundamentalist Christians involved, have historically supported socially conservative policies that they believe exemplify their religious and family values. Key issues for these groups include opposition to abortion and opposition to same-sex marriage, but many Christian conservatives have tended to support conservative fiscal and foreign policy positions as well. In the early 2000s, the Tea Party emerged, a conservative, loosely organized coalition of political groups named partly after the 1773 Boston Tea Party and partly for the "TEA" acronym that signifies the phrase: "taxed enough already." The Tea Party followers generally believe that the federal government has grown too powerful and too fiscally irresponsible, and they push for smaller government, lower taxes, reduced federal debt, and a balanced federal budget. According to a 2012 analysis by author David Brody, the Tea Party has combined with the Evangelical movement to create a new political force that he calls the "Teavangelicals." Brody explains his theory in his book, *The Teavangelicals: The Inside Story of How the Evangelicals and the Tea Party Are Taking Back America.*

The Teavangelical movement, according to Brody, began with the founding of the Moral Majority, a Christian right political organization formed by Reverend Jerry Falwell (1933–2007) in 1979. Falwell was the pastor of the huge Thomas Road Baptist Church in Lynchburg, Virginia. He also was a televangelist who preached on a television program, *Old Time Gospel Hour*. In 1976, Falwell decided to abandon the traditional Baptist position on separating religion and politics and scheduled a series of "I Love America" tours across the United States to raise support for the creation of a national religion-based political organization. The tours proved successful, and Falwell in 1979 created the Moral Majority group to unite and rally religious conservatives to lobby for conservative political causes. Commentators have characterized the Moral Majority as a reaction to what conservatives view as the moral decay of the 1960s—sexual permissiveness, feminism, gay rights, and secularism.

During his time on the national and world stage, Falwell became a prominent political commentator on social issues such as abortion and gay rights. He and his group opposed *Roe v. Wade*, the 1973 Supreme Court case that legalized abortion, and fought against expanding civil rights of gays and lesbians. In 1980, many commentators credited the Moral Majority with helping to elect Republican presidential candidate Ronald Reagan as well as many conservative congressmen. Although the Moral Majority was disbanded about a decade after it began, the influence of the Christian right continued. The Christian Coalition, a political group founded by Pat Robertson, another charismatic televangelist preacher, successfully infiltrated the ranks of the Republican Party, culminating in the 2000 presidential election (and 2004 reelection) of George W. Bush, who reportedly was born again as an evangelical Christian in 1985.

On the one hand, many commentators argue that the Christian right's political influence waned during the Bush administration. Although President Bush established the Office of Faith-Based Initiatives, designed to help faith-based social and charity organizations win millions in federal funding, the Christian right was unable to convince Congress to pass conservative-backed laws that would have allowed state and local governments to become more entwined with religion and permitted churches to directly fund political campaigns. On the other hand, commentators have noted that the religious right was successful in getting President Bush to ban US foreign aid for any family planning organization abroad that either performed legal abortions or provided information about abortion, and in limiting the availability of abortion in US states. Religious lobbyists also continue to push on other political issues, such as allowing creationism to be taught with evolution in school science classes, opposing same-sex marriage, and changing the US Constitution to alter the separation of church and state.

One incarnation of the religious right appears to be within the Tea Party, which began in 2009 largely as a nonreligious protest movement with libertarian political views modeled on those of perennial presidential candidate Ron Paul. Like Ron Paul, early Tea Party protesters generally complained that the federal government has grown too big, that it taxes citizens too much, and that it has taken on too much debt. The Tea Party endorsed a number of candidates to run in the Republican primaries in preparation for the 2010 midterm congressional and state elections, and many of those candidates won, ousting longterm, mainstream Republican incumbents. Between 2009 and 2012, many commentators concluded that the Tea Party had pushed Republican congressional members to become increasingly conservative, especially on fiscal and deficit issues, and had stymied the efforts of Democratic president Barack Obama to find compromises on a range of important matters. In addition, the Tea Party seems to have attracted a wider following made up largely of members of the religious right. According to author David Brody, 50 to 60 percent of Tea Party supporters as of 2012 were conservative Christians. Tea Party fiscal conservatives with evangelical Christians who care deeply about conservative social issues were intent on being a factor in the 2012 presidential and congressional elections, as well as in the future. The authors of the viewpoints included in this chapter debate the central question of what role religion should play in US politics.

Religion and Politics Are Inseparable

Pierre Whalon

Pierre Whalon is the bishop in charge of the Convocation of Episcopal Churches in Europe, based in Paris, France. He is also a columnist and feature writer for both secular and religious publications and blogs.

Cardinal Timothy Dolan appeared on *Face the Nation* on Easter Sunday [2012]. The *New York Times* reported on the conversation.

Asked by . . . [TV moderator Bob] Schieffer if he thought religion was playing too much of a role in politics, the cardinal said, "No, I don't think so at all."

"The public square in the United States is always enriched whenever people approach it when they're inspired by their deepest held convictions," he said. "And, on the other hand, Bob, I think the public square is impoverished when people might be coerced to put a piece of duct tape over their mouth, keeping them from bring[ing] their deepest-held convictions to the conversations."

The cardinal of New York also quashed the idea that one should not vote for [presidential candidate] Mitt Romney just because he is a Mormon.

I agree with him on these two points. I can hear, however, the many people who have walked up to me and told me to keep my preacherly nose out of politics: Nevertheless, it should be clear from human history that religion and politics cannot be separated. Both of them arise from the fact that we *Homo sapiens* are communal beings: we cannot live completely alone.

Every aspect of what makes us human develops completely from living in a community, beginning with the family. Anthropologists are clear that having a sense of the sacred (whatever one makes of it) is one of the fundamental aspects of what differentiates *Sapiens* from other hominids. Politics is how we order our common life.

Can we reasonably expect people not to bring their deepest convictions, which are always religious in nature, to the public square?

It is therefore impossible to separate them, and anyone who claims it can and should be done is either lying or hasn't thought it through. It's pretty basic. . . .

Religion and Politics Intertwined

There are a lot of national elections happening this year around the world. Name one where religion is not a significant factor, even if it is not blaringly obvious, as it is in the United States. France, for instance, will elect a new president next month, and it is clear that Nicolas Sarkozy has been enlisting the help of religious leaders, including Muslims as well as Catholics and Protestants, in his re-election campaign. Just as obviously, his main rival, Socialist François Hollande, has been complaining about Sarkozy's alleged infringements on the *République laïque*, the legally secular, rigorously neutral French Republic. Atheists are religious too.

As a religious leader, I have often been told, as I said, to "stay out of politics." But that is impossible for a Christian, since Jesus of Nazareth's execution—a crucial moment in human history for us—was blatantly political. Proclaiming his Gospel therefore has inevitable political consequences. When Christians began reciting *Kyrie eleison* ("Lord, have mercy") in the liturgy, it was a powerful political statement. That is what a loyal Roman said to Caesar when coming into the emperor's presence. To repeat that in worship clearly states that God, not the emperor or other political ruler, is in charge. Can't get more political than that, especially considering that Caesar was thought to be divine himself.

Along the same lines, examine the places where religion and politics intersect in other faiths. Here, for example, is the right place to question the beliefs of the Mormons if one of them might become the President of the United States. John Kennedy had to answer similar questions, and his Catholicism was not held against him (just as Romney's religion should not stereotype him). The attempts by some Roman Catholic prelates to use excommunication against politicians who support abortion rights raise similar questions, however. Where does faith end and political loyalty begin? Can we reasonably expect people not to bring their deepest convictions, which are always religious in nature, to the public square, as Cardinal Dolan said?

Separation of Church and State

The separation of church and state is certainly a major advance in human history and political theory. Under no circumstances should religious leaders ever be given political power merely because they are part of a religious hierarchy. Iran provides the latest example of how theocracy always corrupts both religion and politics. That said, all of us, even us bishops, have a duty and a right as citizens to engage in politics, at least by casting a vote. In particular, bishops having sworn to guard the faith and unity of the church must speak out from time to time. As Archbishop Rowan Williams has argued, this still has to be done while respecting the relationship between religion and human rights.

This is where I worry about the way in which the Catholic hierarchy, or the Mormon hierarchy for that matter, may try to influence politics. Dolan's call to his fellow bishops to man the barricades on the health care issue does not seem to me to respect the necessary requirement of all religious leaders' sallies into politics. The only way we bishops (or rabbis, or imams, or prophets, etc.) should publicly intervene in the politics of a democratic society is through linking our particular concern to the common good, not the rights of our particular religion. Nor can we argue purely from revelation: why should other citizens respect our opinions if we do not present them as applicable to all people regardless of religion?

As bishop of a multinational jurisdiction in which there is always some election happening, I always call upon the faithful to go and vote. It is biblical that Christians should care about the society we live in (Romans 13:1–7), and in a democracy, voting is a duty. (I also say that if you don't vote, you have no right to complain.) It would be a perversion of my authority to insist that they vote [for] or against particular candidates, though commenting on political ideologies that in my view threaten the common good is not inappropriate. In other words, it's not so much a matter of "do not vote for candidate X" as it is do not support fascism, racism, etc.

There is always a delicate balance to strike. So much is at stake, for all of us. But let us not kid ourselves, at least: religion and politics are inseparable.

Religious Traditions Can Play a Healthy Role in Politics

Robert Jensen

Robert Jensen is an author, a journalism professor at the University of Texas at Austin, and a board member of the Third Coast Activist Resource Center, a community center in Austin, Texas.

Does God take sides in the elections? Is there a voters' guide hiding in our holy books? Should we pray for electoral inspiration?

Secular people tend to answer an emphatic "NO" to those questions, as do most progressive religious folk. Because religious fundamentalists so often present an easy-to-caricature version of faith-based politics—even to the point of implying that God would want us to vote for certain candidates—it is tempting to want to banish all talk of the divine from political life.

But a blanket claim that "religion and politics don't mix" misunderstands the inevitable connection between the two. Whether secular or religious, our political judgments are always rooted in first principles—claims about what it means to be human that can't be reduced to evidence and logic. Should people act purely out of self-interest, or is solidarity with others just as important? Do we owe loyalty to a nation-state? Under what conditions, if any, is the taking of a human life justified? What is the appropriate relationship of human beings to the larger living world?

These basic moral/spiritual questions underlie everyone's politics, and our answers are shaped by the philosophical and/or theological systems in which we find inspiration and insight. Since everyone's political positions reflect their foundational commitments, it doesn't seem fair to say that those grounded in a secular philosophy can draw on their traditions, but people whose political outlooks are rooted in religion have to mute themselves.

The Tradition of Prophecy

Rather than trying to bracket religion out of politics, we should be discussing how religious traditions can play a role in a healthy politics, and one productive place to start in the context of the Christian tradition is [theologian] Walter Brueggemann's new book, *The Practice of Prophetic Imagination: Preaching an Emancipatory Word*. Building on the book for which he is most known—*The Prophetic Imagination*, first published in 1978 with a second edition in 2001—Brueggemann moves beyond sectarian politics and self-satisfied religion to ask difficult questions about our relationship to power. He makes it clear that taking the prophetic tradition seriously means being willing to make those around us—and ourselves—uncomfortable.

In that earlier book, Brueggemann argued that the tradition of prophecy demands more of us than a self-indulgent expression of righteous indignation over injustice or vague calls for social justice, what he calls "a liberal understanding of prophecy" that can serve as "an attractive and face-saving device for any excessive abrasiveness in the service of almost any cause."

Brueggemann wants more from those who claim to stand in the prophetic tradition, which he asserts is rooted in resistance to the dominance of a "royal consciousness" that produces numbness in people. Prophetic ministry, Brueggemann argues in that first book, seeks to "penetrate the numbness in order to face the body of death in which we are caught" and "penetrate despair so that new futures can be believed in and embraced by us." And make no mistake, Brueggemann's concern is not the royal culture of Biblical days but the dominant culture of the contemporary United States and its quest for endless material acquisition and constant expansion of power.

Brueggemann also makes it clear that the prophet is not a finger-wagging scold. The task of prophetic ministry is to bring to public expression "the dread of endings, the collapse of our self-madness, the barriers and pecking orders that secure us at each other's expense, and the fearful practice of eating off the table of a hungry brother or sister." In other words, prophets speak the language of mourning, "that crying in pathos," that provides "the ultimate form of criticism, for it announces the sure end of the whole royal arrangement."

More than three decades after the publication of that book, Brueggemann returns to explore the implications of taking seriously the prophetic imagination, specifically for clergy. But while the book is aimed at preachers and their struggles to bring the prophetic imagination alive in a congregation, Brueggemann's words are relevant to any citizen concerned about the health of our politics and the state of the world.

Contemporary preachers need to connect the dots and make a case that goes against the grain.

The new book begins by arguing that the gospel narrative of social transformation, justice, and compassion is in direct conflict with the dominant narrative of the United States: "therapeutic, technological, consumerist militarism" that "is committed to the notion of self-invention in the pursuit of self-sufficiency." The logic and goals of that dominant culture foster "competitive productivity, motivated by pervasive anxiety about having enough, or being enough, or being in control." All this bolsters notions of "US exceptionalism that gives warrant to the usurpations pursuit of commodities in the name of freedom, at the expense of the neighbor."

Right out of the gate, Brueggemann makes it clear that he is going to critique not just the problems of the moment but the political, economic, and social systems from which those problems emerge, and that to speak frankly about those systems means taking risks. Preachers who put the articulation of this prophetic imagination at the center of their work—and he makes it clear that preachers don't have to claim to be prophets but should see themselves as "handler[s] of the prophetic tradition"—will most likely encounter intense resistance to the message. The dominant narrative does dominate, after all, and critics are rarely embraced.

Just as the prophets struggled to persuade a royal culture that preferred to ignore the message, so do contemporary preachers need to connect the dots and make a case that goes against the grain. Central to this process is that dot-connecting, that naming of reality.

"Prophetic preaching does not put people in crisis. Rather it names and makes palpable the crisis already pulsing among us," Brueggemann writes. "When the dots are connected, it will require naming the defining sins among us of environmental abuse, neighborly disregard, long-term racism, self-indulgent consumerism, all the staples from those ancient truthtellers translated into our time and place."

This is our task—the tearing down of systems inconsistent with our values and the building up of something new, dismantling and restoration.

What masks those sins, Brueggemann writes, is "a totalizing ideology of exceptionalism that precludes critique of our entitlements and self-regard," and the prophetic imagination helps us see that.

Once we accept this critique of the systems that surround us, the next step is dealing with a sense of loss and the accompanying grief as we let go of the illusions that come with wealth and power. "That function of prophetic preaching is important because in a society of buoyant denial as ours is, there is no venue for public grief," he writes. "It is required, in the dominant narrative, to rush past loss to confident 'recovery' according to a tight ideology of success."

Brueggemann does not suggest we stay mired in grief; when society's denial has been penetrated, prophetic preaching has the task of giving voice to "hope-filled possibility." But he reminds us to be careful not to jump too quickly into an empty hope: "Hope can, of course, be spoken too soon. And when spoken too soon, it may too soon overcome the loss and short-circuit the indispensable embrace of guilt and loss. The new possibility is always on the horizon for prophetic preachers. But good sense and theological courage are required to know when to say what."

Brueggemann's analysis may resonate with many progressive people who aren't churchgoers or don't consider themselves spiritual in any sense.

Christian Values Help Solve Political Problems

This is our task—the tearing down of systems inconsistent with our values and the building up of something new, dismantling and restoration—not only for preachers seeking to be handlers of the prophetic tradition, but for anyone interested in facing honestly our political, economic, and social problems. The task, in Brueggemann's words, is "to mediate a relinquishment of a world that is gone and a reception of a world that is being given."

Again, Brueggemann's goal in the book isn't to advocate for specific politicians, parties, or political programs, but to articulate the underlying values that should inform our political thinking. He seeks to confront truth (against denial) and articulate hope (against despair) in the face of a "denying, despairing, totalizing ideology" that presents itself as the only game in town. While it is difficult for many people to let go of the dominant ideology, Brueggemann argues that people "yearn and trust for more than the empire can offer. We yearn for abundance and transformation and restoration. We yearn beyond the possible."

Brueggemann's analysis may resonate with many progressive people who aren't churchgoers or don't consider themselves spiritual in any sense, but who may ask whether his arguments need to draw on a religious tradition. Wouldn't most of his arguments make just as much sense in the language of secular politics? I think they would, but there is great value in Brueggemann's approach.

Rather than closing down conversation along sectarian lines, our religious traditions have the capacity to open up the conversations about meaning that are difficult to have in a privatized, depoliticized, mass-mediated, mass-medicated world.

First, whatever any one person's beliefs, the dominant religion in the United States is Christianity; around three-quarters of the US population identifies as Christian in some sense. The stories of that tradition are the stories of our culture, and the struggle over that interpretation is crucial to political and social life.

Even more important is the fact that church is still a place where people come to think about these basic questions. Even in the most timid church, the question of "what are people for?" is on the agenda, and hence there is potential to challenge the dominant culture's values.

"The local congregation continues to be a matrix for emancipatory, subversive utterance that is not amenable to totalizing ideology," Brueggemann writes. "People continue to sit and listen attentively to the exposition of the word. People still entertain the odd thought, in spite of the reductionisms of modernity, that God is a real character and the defining agent in the life of the world. People still gather in church to hear and struggle with what is not on offer anywhere else."

Brueggemann's invocation of "God" may put off secular people, who assume that any use of the term implies super-natural claims about God as an actual being that directs the universe. But that is not the only way to understand God, of course. In fact, one of the greatest conversation-starting aspects of this approach is the always provocative question, "What do you mean by God?" When someone cites God, we can—and should—ask: Is God a being, entity, or force in the world? Is God the name humans use for that which is beyond our understanding? What is God to you? Rather than closing down conversation along sectarian lines, our religious traditions have the capacity to open up the conversations about meaning that are difficult to have in a privatized, depoliticized, mass-mediated, mass-medicated world.

To ask whether we should understand our world through a religious or secular lens is to misunderstand both—it's not an either/or proposition. We have the tools of modernity and science to help us understand what we can understand about the material world. We have faith traditions that remind us of the limits of our understanding. In the church I attend (a progressive Presbyterian congregation, St. Andrew's) those two approaches are not at odds but part of the same project—to understand a world facing multiple crises, drawing on the best of religious and secular traditions, struggling together to solve the problems that can be solved and to face the problems that may be beyond solutions.

In a world in collapse, these realities often seem too painful to bear and the work before us often seems overwhelming. The prophetic tradition offers a language for understanding that pain and finding the collective strength to continue.

Religious Fundamentalism Has Transformed Conservative Politics into a Religious Jihad

Neal Gabler

Neal Gabler is a professor, journalist, author, film critic, and political commentator, as well as a senior fellow at the University of Southern California Annenberg Norman Lear Center, a research and public policy organization.

For decades now, liberals have been agonizing because conservatives seem to win even when polls show that the public generally disagrees with them. In their postmortems, liberals have placed blame on the way they frame their message, or on the right-wing media drumbeat that drowns out everything else, or on the right's co-opting of the flag, Mom and apple pie, which is designed to make liberals seem like effete, hostile foreign agents.

It's understandable that liberals prefer to think of their subordination as a matter of their own inadequacies or of conservative wiles. Theoretically, you can learn how to improve your message or how to match wits with adversaries, and a lot of liberal hand-wringing has been dedicated to doing just that. But it is becoming increasingly clear that liberals haven't just been succumbing to superior message control, or even to a superior political narrative (conservatives' frontier individualism versus liberals' communitarianism). They are up against something far more intractable and far more difficult to defeat. They are up against religion.

Neal Gabler, "Politics as Religion in America," *Los Angeles Times*, October 2, 2009. Copyright © 2009 by The Los Angeles Times. All rights reserved. Reproduced by permission.

The Transformation of Conservatism into Religion

Perhaps the single most profound change in our political culture over the last 30 years has been the transformation of conservatism from a political movement, with all the limitations, hedges and forbearances of politics, into a kind of fundamentalist religious movement, with the absolute certainty of religious belief.

I don't mean "religious belief" literally. This transformation is less a function of the alliance between Protestant evangelicals, their fellow travelers and the right (though that alliance has had its effect) than it is a function of a belief in one's own rightness so unshakable that it is not subject to political caveats. In short, what we have in America today is a political fundamentalism, with all the characteristics of religious fundamentalism and very few of the characteristics of politics.

The tea-baggers who hate President Obama . . . honestly believe that the political system . . . is broken and only can be fixed by substituting their certainty for the uncertainties of American politics.

For centuries, American democracy as a process of conflict resolution has been based on give-and-take; negotiation; compromise; the acceptance of the fact that the majority rules, with respect for minority rights; and, above all, on an agreement to abide by the results of a majority vote. It takes compromise, even defeat, in stride because it is a fluid system. As historian Arthur Schlesinger Jr. once put it, the beauty of a democracy is that the minority always has the possibility of becoming the majority.

Religious fundamentalism, on the other hand, rests on immutable truths that cannot be negotiated, compromised or changed. In this, it is diametrically opposed to liberal democracy as we have practiced it in America. Democrats of every political stripe may defend democracy to the death, but very few would defend individual policies to the death. You don't wage bloody crusades for banking regulation or the minimum wage or even healthcare reform. When politics becomes religion, however, policy too becomes a matter of life and death, as we have all seen.

That is one reason our founding fathers opted for a separation of church and state. They recognized that religion and politics could coexist only when they occupied different domains. Most denominations, which preach and practice tolerance, have rendered unto Caesar what is Caesar's. Religious groups may have found a community of interest with a political party to further their aims; they have not, by and large, sought to convert the political system into a religious one. Until now.

You cannot convince religious fanatics of anything other than what they already believe, even if their religion is political dogma.

The tea-baggers who hate President [Barack] Obama with a fervor that is beyond politics; the fear-mongers who warn that Obama is another Hitler or Stalin; the wannabe storm troopers who brandish their guns and warn darkly of the president's demise; the cable and talk-radio blowhards who make a living out of demonizing Obama and tarring liberals as America-haters—these people are not just exercising their rights within the political system. They honestly believe that the political system—a system that elected Obama—is broken and only can be fixed by substituting their certainty for the uncertainties of American politics.

A Losing Battle

As we are sadly discovering, this minority cannot be headed off, which is most likely why conservatism transmogrified from politics to a religion in the first place. Conservatives who sincerely believed that theirs is the only true and right path have come to realize that political tolerance is no match for religious vehemence.

Unfortunately, they are right. Having opted out of political discourse, they are not susceptible to any suasion. Rationality won't work because their arguments are faith-based rather than evidence-based. Better message control won't work. Improved strategies won't work. Grass-roots organizing won't work. Nothing will work because you cannot convince religious fanatics of anything other than what they already believe, even if their religion is political dogma.

And therein lies the problem, not only for liberals but for mainstream conservatives who think of conservatism as an ideology, not an orthodoxy. You cannot beat religion with politics, which is why the extreme right "wins" so many battles. The fundamentalist political fanatics will always be more zealous than mainstream conservatives or liberals. They will always be louder, more adamant, more aggrieved, more threatening, more willing to do anything to win. Losing is inconceivable. For them, every battle is a crusade—or a jihad—a matter of good and evil.

There is something terrifying in this. The media have certainly been cowed; they treat intolerance as if it were legitimate political activity. So have many politicians, and not just the conservative ones who know that if they don't fall in line, they will be run over. This political fundamentalism has also invaded the general culture in deleterious ways. The ugly incivility of recent months is partly the result of political fundamentalists who have nothing but contempt for opposing viewpoints, which gives them license to shout down opponents or threaten them, just as jihadis everywhere do.

Those who oppose the religification of politics may think all they have to do is change tactics, but they are sadly, tragically mistaken. They can never win, because for the political fundamentalists, this isn't political jousting, this is Armageddon.

With stakes like that, they will not lose, and there is nothing democrats—small 'd' and capital "D"—can do about it.

What Role Should Religion Play in Politics, Judicial Decisions and Laws?

Brian Faller

Brian Faller is an attorney and a member of the board of contributors for The Olympian, *a newspaper in Olympia, Washington.*

Is it appropriate that judges, politicians or voters make decisions and publicly justify those decisions based on religious texts?

For example, would it be objectionable that passages from the Bible or the Quran serve as a legal justification for laws that criminalize abortion?

The United States Constitution provides for a separation of church and state. It prohibits laws "respecting an establishment of religion" and laws applying a religious test for eligibility to hold a public office. At the same time, the Constitution secures the "free exercise" of religion so that people can believe and practice (or not) a faith of their choice.

This separation of church and state protects the citizen from having the religious views of others imposed on them by coercive law or by legislation of a religious concept of the good. It thus protects a pluralism of religions and moral views against theocracy and the civil strife it leads to when government enforces a religion on unwilling citizens.

The doctrine of separation also reflects the fact that religious beliefs are traditionally based upon asserted revealed truths that a significant segment of other believers and nonbelievers reasonably do not accept as reliable sources or truths.

Indeed, religious followers often interpret the same religious texts to reach vastly different conclusions, and in modern society, numerous commands in religious books such as stoning prostitutes to death, amputating hands of thieves, and beating disobedient children, are proscribed.

Clearly citizens (and politicians) are free under our Constitution to argue for laws based on religion and could not be punished for doing so. However, the question here is not one of legal duty, but of a civic duty which is an ideal not enforceable by law, like the duty to vote.

If politicians and citizens publicly accept religious justifications for law, the pressure would mount for judges (who are appointed by politicians or elected by citizens) to follow.

Many political philosophers argue that to preserve pluralistic democracy, citizens and politicians should recognize a civic duty to base their votes and public justification of coercive laws on neutral grounds, such as shared values and factual considerations, rather than revealed religious truths or one's comprehensive moral view. Such a view does not exclude values found in religion or moral theory from the public debate where such values are shared among reasonable persons.

The abortion dispute can provide an example how neutral grounds work. The public abortion debate might be recast in non-religious terms, shifting the focus from a religious designation of an embryo/early fetus as a person or human being to considerations of fact, such as whether and to what extent an embryo/early fetus has thoughts, memories, expectations, a sense of loss, differentiates self from world, acts, experiences pain from abortion, resembles a human, etc., whether and to what extent our shared values give moral weight to the potential of an organism to develop characteristics of mature humans, whether and to what extent prohibition will result in deaths of mothers from illegal abortions and in childbirth, whether and to what extent children who would have been aborted will be adequately cared for, whether and to what extent allowing abortion will lead to societal acceptance of infanticide, euthanasia, or mistreatment of humans with mental or physical challenges, etc.

No doubt I have left off a number of important considerations in the abortion debate, but this list illustrates how controversial issues can at least in part be addressed by identifying and weighing factual outcomes and shared values.

Indeed, neutral grounds are themselves used to justify this civic duty. If politicians and citizens publicly accept religious justifications for law, the pressure would mount for judges (who are appointed by politicians or elected by citizens) to follow. And if politicians and citizens publicly justify their votes on nonreligious grounds but actually vote based on religious grounds, it would at times result in hypocritical laws silently justified on religious grounds.

To me, these considerations suggest that we should recognize a civic duty to base our votes and public justifications of coercive laws on neutral, nonreligious grounds, because doing so provides a critical bulwark to safeguard pluralistic democracy from creeping theocracy.

A Majority of Americans Think Churches Should Stay Out of Politics

The Pew Forum on Religion & Public Life

The Pew Forum on Religion & Public Life is a project of the Pew Research Center, a nonpartisan research and polling organization that provides information on the issues, attitudes, and trends affecting the United States and the world.

A new survey finds signs of public uneasiness with the mixing of religion and politics. The number of people who say there has been too much religious talk by political leaders stands at an all-time high since the Pew Research Center began asking the question more than a decade ago. And most Americans continue to say that churches and other houses of worship should keep out of politics.

Survey Results

Nearly four-in-ten Americans (38%) now say there has been too much expression of religious faith and prayer from political leaders, while 30% say there has been too little. In 2010, more said there was too little than too much religious expression from politicians (37% vs. 29%). The percentage saying there is too much expression of religious faith by politicians has increased across party lines, but this view remains far more widespread among Democrats than Republicans.

Slightly more than half of the public (54%) says that churches should keep out of politics, compared with 40% who say religious institutions should express their views on social and political matters. This is the third consecutive poll conducted over the past four years in which more people have said churches and other houses of worship should keep out of politics than said they should express their views on social and political topics. By contrast, between 1996 and 2006 the balance of opinion on this question consistently tilted in the opposite direction.

These are among the findings from the latest national survey by the Pew Research Center for the People & the Press and the Pew Research Center's Forum on Religion & Public Life, conducted March 7–11 among 1,503 adults. While there are substantial partisan differences over religion and politics, the survey finds there also are divisions within the GOP [Republican] primary electorate.

51% of the public say that religious conservatives have too much control over the Republican Party.

Nearly six-in-ten (57%) Republican and Republican-leaning voters who favor Mitt Romney for the Republican nomination say churches should keep out of political matters. By contrast, 60% of GOP voters who support Rick Santorum say that churches and other houses of worship should express their views on social and political questions.

And while 55% of Santorum's supporters say there is too little expression of religious faith and prayer by political leaders, just 24% of Romney's backers agree, while 33% say there is too much expression of faith and prayer by politicians.

The new survey finds that more people view the GOP as friendly to religion than say the same about the Democratic Party, a pattern observed for much of the past decade.

At the same time, 51% of the public say that religious conservatives have too much control over the Republican

Party. Fewer express the view that liberals who are not religious have too much control over the Democratic Party (41%).

Opinions about whether the [Barack] Obama administration is friendly toward religion have shifted modestly since 2009. Currently, 39% say the administration is friendly to religion, 32% say it is neutral and 23% say it is unfriendly. The balance of opinion was comparable in August 2009, although somewhat fewer (17%) said the administration was unfriendly to religion.

However, there has been a noticeable shift in opinions among white Catholics, perhaps reflecting effects from the controversy over the administration's policies on contraception coverage. The percentage of white Catholics who say the administration is unfriendly to religion has nearly doubled— from 17% to 31%—since 2009. Three years ago, far more white Catholics said the administration was friendly (35%) than unfriendly to religion (17%); today, nearly as many say the administration is unfriendly (31%) as friendly (38%).

Expressions of Faith by Political Leaders

A plurality of the public (38%) says that there has been too much expression of religious faith and prayer from political leaders, while 30% say there has been too little religious expression and 25% say there has been the right amount of discussion of religion from political leaders. The number saying there has been too much religious talk from political leaders now stands at its highest point since the Pew Research Center began asking the question more than a decade ago.

Since October 2001, shortly after the 9/11 attacks, the rise in the number saying there has been too much religious expression by political leaders has been most pronounced among Democrats and independents. Nearly half of Democrats (46%) now say there has been too much discussion of religious faith and prayer by politicians, as do 42% of independents.

The number of Republicans expressing unease with the amount of politicians' religious talk also has increased (from 8% in 2001 to 24% currently). But Republicans have consistently been less inclined than either Democrats or independents to say there has been too much religious talk from political leaders.

Since 2010, there have been sizable increases in the percentages of white mainline Protestants, white Catholics and the religiously unaffiliated saying that there has been too much discussion of religion by political leaders.

However, there has been no change in opinions among white evangelical Protestants, who remain far less likely than those in other religious groups to say that politicians express religious faith too much.

Roughly half of college graduates (49%) now say there has been too much religious discussion from political leaders, up 14 points since 2010. Those with some college education have also become increasingly uncomfortable with the amount of religious expression from political leaders, with 38% now saying there has been too much religion talk from politicians (up from 27% in 2010). By contrast, there has been little change in opinion on this question among those with a high school degree or less education.

White evangelical Protestants . . . remain far less likely than those in other religious groups to say that politicians express religious faith too much.

Views of Churches' Involvement in Politics

A majority of Americans (54%) say that churches and other houses of worship should keep out of political matters, while 40% say they should express their views on social and political questions. After a decade in which the balance of opinion tilted in the opposite direction, this is the third consecutive survey in the past four years in which more people say churches should keep out of politics than say churches should express their views on social and political issues.

When this question was first asked by the Pew Research Center in 1996, there was little partisan division. Roughly four-in-ten Republicans and independents said churches should keep out of politics (42% each), as did 44% of Democrats. Currently, 44% of Republicans say churches should stay out of politics, compared with 60% of Democrats and 58% of independents.

Majorities of the religiously unaffiliated . . . say churches and other houses of worship should steer clear of politics.

There also are significant divisions on this issue among religious groups. A majority of white evangelical Protestants (60%) say that churches and other houses of worship should express their views on social and political issues. The views of this group have changed little since 2006, even as the public as a whole has increasingly taken the view that religious institutions should keep out of politics.

Black Protestants are divided on this question, with 51% saying churches should express their views and 43% saying they should keep out of politics. By contrast, in July 2006, 69% of black Protestants said churches and other houses of worship should express their views on social and political issues.

Majorities of the religiously unaffiliated (66%), Catholics (60%) and white mainline Protestants (60%) say churches and other houses of worship should steer clear of politics.

Political Parties' Friendliness to Religion

A majority of the public (54%) views the Republican Party as friendly to religion, while 24% say the GOP is neutral to religion and 13% say it is unfriendly toward religion. Roughly four-in-ten (39%) rate the Obama administration as friendly, with 32% saying it is neutral and 23% saying the administration is unfriendly to religion. The Democratic Party is seen as friendly to religion by 35% of the public; it is seen as neutral by 36% and as unfriendly by 21% of the public.

Approximately one-in-five Americans (19%) rate news reporters and the news media as friendly to religion, and 14% say university professors are friendly to religion. Roughly one-in-three say that reporters (35%) and professors (32%) are unfriendly to religion.

Over the past decade, the Republican Party has consistently been seen as friendly to religion by more people than has the Democratic Party. The current poll finds a significant rebound since 2010 in the number describing both parties as friendly to religion.

The increase in the percentage viewing the GOP as friendly to religion has been broad-based. Nearly two-thirds of Republicans (65%) describe the GOP as friendly to religion, up eight points since 2010, as do roughly half (54%) of political independents, up 12 points. Among Democrats, 48% now view the GOP as friendly to religion, compared with 36% who said this in 2010.

The number of people saying the Obama administration is friendly to religion is steady compared with 2009.

The rise in the number saying the Democratic Party is friendly to religion is concentrated among Democrats and independents. A clear majority of Democrats (57%) now view their party as friendly to religion, up 15 points since 2010. The percentage of independents describing the Democratic Party as friendly to religion now stands at 29%, up from 20% in 2010.

The Obama Administration and Religion

A plurality of the public (39%) says the Obama administration is friendly to religion, while 32% say the administration is neutral toward religion and 23% say it is unfriendly to religion. A majority of Democrats (59%) say the administration is friendly to religion, while about half of Republicans polled say it is unfriendly toward religion. Independents are evenly divided between those who view the administration as friendly to religion (36%) and those who see it as neutral toward religion (38%); 21% of independents see the Obama administration as unfriendly to religion.

These partisan leanings are reflected in the views of religious groups. A plurality of white evangelicals (44%) views the administration as unfriendly toward religion, while two-thirds of black Protestants (65%) say it is friendly toward religion.

The number of people saying the Obama administration is friendly to religion is steady compared with 2009, when this question was last asked. But over the same period of time, there has been a small but noticeable increase in the number saying the Obama administration is unfriendly to religion (from 17% in 2009 to 23% today). This change is concentrated exclusively among Republicans, among whom half (52%) now view the Obama administration as unfriendly to religion.

The number of Catholics describing the Obama administration as unfriendly to religion has risen 10-percentage points since 2009 (from 15% to 25%); among white Catholics, roughly one-third (31%) now view the administration as unfriendly to religion, up 14 points since 2009. There also has been a significant increase in the percentage of the religiously unaffiliated who view the Obama administration as unfriendly to religion.

49

Reporters, Professors, and Religion

About a third of the public (32%) perceives university professors as unfriendly to religion, while 37% describe professors as neutral to religion; far fewer (14%) say university professors are generally friendly toward religion. Compared with 2003 (when this question was last asked), there has been a noticeable rise in the number describing professors as unfriendly to religion and a slight downturn in the number saying professors are friendly to religion.

College graduates are more apt than those with less education to describe professors as neutral toward religion, while more of those who have not graduated from college express no opinion on this question.

A majority of Republicans (56%) say that professors are unfriendly toward religion. By contrast, a plurality of Democrats (46%) says that professors are neutral toward religion. Among independents, 37% say professors are neutral toward religion, while 31% describe them as unfriendly and 16% say they are friendly to religion.

Among white evangelicals surveyed, 56% view professors as unfriendly toward religion. Among most other religious groups, pluralities or majorities describe professors as either neutral or friendly toward religion.

Independents, by a wide margin . . . say that religious conservatives have too much influence over the GOP.

Roughly a third (35%) of the public says that news reporters and the news media are unfriendly toward religion, while 38% describe reporters as neutral to religion and 19% describe the media as friendly toward religion. The number saying news reporters are friendly toward religion has increased slightly compared with 2009, whereas the number describing the media as neutral toward religion has ticked down since then.

A majority of Republicans (56%) see the media as unfriendly to religion, while most Democrats and independents say reporters are neutral or friendly to religion. About half of white evangelicals in the survey (53%) say reporters and the news media are unfriendly toward religion. Among other religious groups, half or more rate the news media as neutral or friendly to religion.

Religious Conservatives Seen as Having Too Much Control over GOP

About half of the public (51%) agrees that religious conservatives have too much control over the GOP. Fewer (41%) agree that liberals who are not religious have too much control over the Democratic Party. These opinions are little changed from August 2008, during the last presidential campaign.

Partisans break along predictable lines in views of the influences over their own party and the opposing party. Independents, by a wide margin (57% to 42%), are more likely than to say that religious conservatives have too much influence over the GOP than that secular liberals have too much sway over the Democratic Party.

The religiously unaffiliated stand out as the religious group most inclined to think that religious conservatives have too much sway in the GOP, with 66% expressing this view. Roughly half of white mainline Protestants (53%) and white Catholics (56%) say the same. By contrast, 56% of white evangelicals disagree that religious conservatives have too much power in the GOP.

The belief that secular liberals have too much control over the Democratic Party is most pronounced among white evangelicals (58%). White mainline Protestants, white Catholics and black Protestants are divided on this question, while the large majority of the religiously unaffiliated (64%) rejects the idea that secular liberals have too much power over the Democratic Party.

CHAPTER 2

Does Government Interfere with Religious Freedom?

Chapter Preface

One of the persistent myths about the United States is that it has always been a land of religious tolerance. Presidents from George Washington to Barack Obama have lauded the country's commitment to religious freedom, its embrace of all religious beliefs, and its secular government. The truth is a very different story, one of religious persecution of minority religions, battles among various religious sects, animosity toward unbelievers and native religions, and governmental sanctions of favored religions.

Many Americans are familiar with the history of the Puritans who fled religious persecution in England and established settlements in North America in the 1600s, but this well-known story is only part of the country's early history. Although the Puritans experienced persecution themselves and saw its injustice, they mostly failed to treat other religions with the tolerance or acceptance they sought for themselves. Certain of their faith, the Puritans made their chosen religious beliefs the foundation of their communities' civic government. Believers in other religions, like Catholics or Quakers, were banned from Puritan settlements in the Boston area, and in some cases these individuals were attacked or hanged for asserting their religious beliefs.

The local and state governments that formed in early North America also favored some religions over others and discriminated against certain religious groups. In Massachusetts, for example, Catholics were forbidden from holding public office unless they renounced their loyalty to the pope. Similarly, New York State's constitution initially banned Catholics from public office, and other states such as Maryland approved of Catholics but not Jews. A number of states also had state-sanctioned and state-supported churches. Even Virginia, home of founding father Thomas Jefferson, considered legislation that would have linked the state government with Christian religions, but this step was avoided when the state legislature instead passed Jefferson's plan calling for freedom of religion and separation of church and state.

Thomas Jefferson's vision of religious freedom and tolerance eventually became part of the 1776 US Constitution. Article VI provides that no religious test can ever be required as a qualification for any public office, and the First Amendment contains a guarantee of religious freedom and a prohibition against government establishment of religion. However, these constitutional protections were violated in the years that followed.

Beginning in the colonial period, for example, Catholics experienced many forms of discrimination, including legislation that limited their rights and freedoms. Catholics were often barred from public office, excluded from certain professions, denied voting rights, and prevented from owning land or property. In some cases, parents were fined for sending their children to Catholic schools. Prejudice against Catholics slowly subsided in the United States in the modern era, but it was still a factor in 1960 when John F. Kennedy, a Catholic, ran for president.

Similarly, during the nineteenth and much of the twentieth centuries, Jews were routinely discriminated against in employment, schools, social clubs, and other arenas. Anti-Semitism peaked in the 1920s and 1930s and then slowly waned after World War II, after millions of Jews immigrated to the United States from Eastern Europe and, like other immigrant groups, gradually integrated into US society and the US economy.

Mormons, too, were persecuted by many Americans, especially in the nineteenth century, when acts of violence were sometimes directed against Mormon communities. In Missouri, for example, following a battle between Mormons and the state militia, Governor Lilburn Boggs in 1833 issued an extermination order, forcing Mormons to leave the state. The Mormon sect also met opposition in Illinois, where its founder Joseph Smith was murdered. Eventually, Mormons settled in what is now Utah. Times have changed significantly since the 1800s, but Mitt Romney, a Mormon presidential candidate in the 2012 presidential election, nevertheless found his faith to be a topic of much interest and debate.

In the early 2000s, Muslims living in the United States came under attack, following the terrorist attacks of September 11, 2001. Moreover, the focus on terrorists who follow a militant or radical form of Islam caused many American Christians to see all Muslims as violent extremists. Peaceful American Muslims have suffered as a result, enduring hate speech, suspicions that they are terrorists, and attacks on their mosques. In 2010, a controversy began over the building of an Islamic community center in New York City near Ground Zero, the location of the World Trade Center buildings that were targeted by terrorists on 9/11. Protests erupted around the United States, and many argued that Muslims should not be permitted to build the center so close to the memorial site because it would disrespect the people killed in the attack. The controversy eased after New York mayor Michael Bloomberg and President Barack Obama stood up for the rights of Muslims, and the Islamic center opened quietly in September 2011.

This trend of Islamophobia coincides with the insistence among various Christian groups that the federal government infringes on their religious freedom. The authors of the viewpoints included in this chapter discuss whether the United States and other governments are interfering with religious freedom.

President Barack Obama's Health Insurance Mandate Violates the Religious Beliefs of Catholic Institutions

Mike Brownfield

Mike Brownfield is assistant director of strategic communications at The Heritage Foundation, a conservative think tank, and he is editor of The Foundry, *Heritage's public policy news blog, and* The Morning Bell, *the group's e-newsletter.*

It has not even been two years since Obamacare was enacted, and already the President's health care law has taken another victim—the religious freedoms Americans hold dear, as reflected by the First Amendment.

The Contraception Rule

The [Barack] Obama Administration recently reaffirmed a rule under Obamacare that requires many religious employers to provide health care coverage for all FDA [Food and Drug Administration]-approved contraceptive methods, sterilization procedures, and related education and counseling. On the grounds that certain FDA-approved contraceptive methods can sometimes "cause the demise of embryos both after and before uterine implantation," many groups also believe that the rule forces them to cover abortion.

The United States Conference of Catholic Bishops is calling the contraception mandate an "unprecedented" attack on religious freedom. And in statement after statement issued in diocese after diocese, many bishops are publicly declaring that they "cannot" and "will not" comply with "this unjust law." As Cleveland Bishop Richard Lennon explained, "Unless this rule is overturned, Catholics will be compelled either to violate our consciences or to drop health care coverage for our employees."

The Obama Administration has imposed its will on the very institutions the First Amendment sought to protect.

It's not just Catholics affected by the rule, however. Leaders from other faith traditions have expressed their concern, and the Becket Fund for Religious Liberty has already filed a lawsuit on behalf of an interdenominational Christian college that objects to providing abortion and related education and counseling in its health care insurance. "The mandate is un-American, unprecedented, and flagrantly unconstitutional," says an attorney for the college.

As shocking as the Obama Administration's action is, it should not come as a surprise. Heritage [Foundation] experts explained years ago that freedom of conscience in health care is closely linked to greater personal freedom over health care decisions. Health care expert James Capretta says that "it was inevitable—only a matter of time," now that the government is calling the shots and making health care choices for the American people. "Just the sight of Catholic leaders' being forced to go begging before federal officials ought to be enough to convince most Americans that handing over so much power over such sensitive matters to the federal government was a terrible, terrible mistake," he writes.

This erosion of fundamental religious freedoms at the hands of the Obamacare bureaucracy is the sort of clash of government versus religious freedom that the Founders foresaw when, in the First Amendment of the Constitution, they prescribed that "Congress shall make no law respecting an establishment of religion, or prohibiting the free exercise thereof." Not withstanding that prohibition, the Obama Administration has imposed its will on the very institutions the First Amendment sought to protect. Though the rule provides a narrow exemption for "houses of worship," it unfortunately burdens their affiliated institutions, schools, and hospitals—thereby violating the freedom of religion. David Addington, Vice President of Domestic and Economic Policy at The Heritage Foundation, explains that the Obama Administration should take action to exempt these institutions and preserve their religious liberty:

> The Department of Health and Human Services should broadly exempt religious institutions in its final regulations implementing the Obamacare contraception mandate, pending repeal of that mandate as part of the Obamacare statute repeal. Such an exemption would allow the religious institutions both to adhere, as they must, to the tenets of their faiths and to provide group health care plans for their employees. Absent such an exemption, many religious institutions, following their faiths, will have no alternative but to stop making group health plans available to their employees and pay any fines for failure to do so.
>
> Surely President Obama did not intend what he considers his signature legislative achievement to trample on freedom of religion and to result in the loss of group health care coverage for employees of religious institutions. This is, after all, the man who told us all in 2006 that "secularists are wrong when they ask believers to leave their religion at the door before entering into the public square."

New York Archbishop Timothy Dolan cautioned, "This latest erosion of our first freedom should make all Americans pause. When the government tampers with a freedom so fundamental to the life of our nation, one shudders to think what lies ahead." Those dire words of warning sadly ring true. Obamacare was designed to place total power in the hands of the federal government—in an unelected bureaucracy with the power to dictate the operation of an industry that is fundamental to Americans' health and wellbeing. With this decision, the Obama Administration has demonstrated just how far that power can go, what freedoms it can take away, and why this law must be repealed.

The US Government Has Taken a Number of Actions That Restrict Religious Freedom

Sarah Pulliam Bailey

Sarah Pulliam Bailey is the online editor for Christianity Today, *a religious magazine.*

The past year [2011] has marked a shift in religious liberty debates, one that previously centered on hiring rights but became focused on health care requirements. When President [Barack] Obama first took office [January 2009], faith-based groups were especially concerned that organizations that discriminate in hiring based on religious beliefs would become ineligible for federal funding. In 2011, the President indicated that he would not rescind an executive order on hiring rights. Just a week later, though, Health and Human Services ruled that religious groups other than churches must provide their employees contraception, triggering lawsuits and petitions. But contraception is not the only religious freedom issue faith-based groups are eyeing. The following timeline shows a number of actions the government took in the past year, setting precedents and priorities on various issues, including sexual orientation, health care, and hiring decisions.

Health care workers and the 'conscience clause'

February 18, 2011: The Obama administration revises "conscience clause" rules, maintaining the provision that allows workers to refrain from performing abortions but calling the Bush-enacted rule "unclear and potentially overbroad in scope." The earlier provision was interpreted as allowing such workers to opt out of a broad range of medical services, such as providing Plan B or other contraception.

Defense of Marriage Act

February 23, 2011: President Obama announced that the federal government would no longer defend the constitutionality of the Defense of Marriage Act. The move stemmed from the administration's decision that sexual orientation should be protected by the highest legal scrutiny afforded by the 14th Amendment. Neither the Supreme Court nor federal law has added sexual orientation to the list of characteristics especially protected against discrimination, like race, gender, or national origin. But the administration's efforts to add it could set a precedent. Many observers believe such an inclusion would allow the government to invoke a "compelling government interest" in forbidding faith-based organizations from considering some sexual ethics questions in employment decisions.

Prisons

April 13, 2011: The Justice Department files a lawsuit against a county in South Carolina where a South Carolina sheriff was prohibiting inmates from getting devotional materials. The county eventually agreed to let inmates receive religious materials.

National Day of Prayer and courts

April 14, 2011: A federal appeals court dismisses a lawsuit against the National Day of Prayer, overturning a 2010 U.S. District ruling that the day was unconstitutional, which the Justice Department appealed. Obama had discontinued President Bush's annual observances at the White House, but issued a proclamation on the 2011 National Day of Prayer.

Hiring rights and federal funding

July 25, 2011: Comments from President Obama suggested that he does not plan to change an executive order that permits some faith-based organizations that receive federal funding to discriminate in hiring based on applicants' religious beliefs. Obama maintained a position in an executive order that states that while federally-funded religious organizations cannot discriminate against beneficiaries, they may retain religious hiring practices.

Contraception and religious exemption

August 1, 2011: The Department of Health and Human Services announced that employers must provide contraceptives (including those that block uterine implantation) in insurance plans. Churches are exempt from the mandate, but not religious employers, such as soup kitchens, homeless shelters, parachurch ministries, religious hospitals, and religious universities. The ruling triggers petitions and requests for a stronger religious exemption, including a lawsuit from Colorado Christian University.

Chaplains and 'Don't Ask Don't Tell'

September 20, 2011: The military ended its "don't ask, don't tell" policy on gays and lesbians serving openly in the military. The Pentagon also issued a memo allowing military chaplains to perform same-sex marriages if it is allowed by the law and the chaplain's beliefs.

The United States Agency for International Development (USAID) began inserting new language in its mandatory requirements, saying that it "strongly encourages" all grant applicants to adopt USAID's hiring policy of not discriminating on the basis of sexual orientation.

Hiring rights and discrimination

October 5, 2011: As the Supreme Court considered *Hosanna-Tabor v. EEOC*, an employment dispute at a Lutheran school, the administration argued that the First Amendment's religion clauses do not exempt churches from employment discrimination laws, even when considering head clergy. (Though the administration did allow that the right of expressive association might be compromised by such laws.)

In January 2012, a unanimous Court rejected the administration's argument as untenable, saying, "We cannot accept the remarkable view that the Religion Clauses have nothing to say about a religious organization's freedom to select its own ministers."

Hiring rights and sexual orientation

October 11, 2011: The United States Agency for International Development (USAID) began inserting new language in its mandatory requirements, saying that it "strongly encourages" all grant applicants to adopt USAID's hiring policy of not discriminating on the basis of sexual orientation. Christian aid groups like World Vision opposed the language and unsuccessfully asked for additional language clarifying that religious employers retain rights to consider religion in hiring. USAID says the policy is not binding and White House officials suggest dialogue on the issue will continue.

Federal funding and sex trafficking

October 2011: Health and Human Services [HHS] defunded the U.S. Conference of Catholic Bishops' [USCCB] domestic program to assist and resettle human trafficking victims. More than 20 U.S. senators wrote a letter to HHS requesting an explanation. The USCCB believes its program was defunded because of its religious opposition to providing abortions or contraceptives to trafficked women.

Discrimination and hiring rights

December 6, 2011: President Obama issued a memorandum announcing that ending discrimination against those who are gay "is central to the United States commitment to promoting human rights" and "directing all agencies engaged abroad to ensure that U.S. diplomacy and foreign assistance promote and protect the human rights of LGBT [lesbian, gay, bisexual, and trangendered] persons." On December 16, a dozen faith-based groups who engage in international relief and development sent a private letter to Obama, urging him to clarify to agencies that his directive does not affect religious organizations' hiring rights. The letter asked him to clarify that his memo would not mandate a new LGBT "litmus test" for indigenous groups that the organizations partner with in international relief work. The White House did not reply to the group's letter.

Contraception and national security

December 19, 2011: President Obama signed an executive order declaring women's access to reproductive healthcare during conflict and humanitarian emergencies a matter of U.S. national security. It is unclear whether the declaration will be cited as evidence that there would be a compelling government interest in compelling federal grantees to distribute emergency contraceptives that block uterine implantation.

Contraception and religious exemption

January 20, 2012: Health and Human Services announced that it will not expand the religious exemption for the August contraception ruling beyond churches, sparking further concern from religious groups. Secretary Kathleen Sebelius extends the enforcement of the mandate to 2013.

Contraception and cost

February 10, 2012: President Obama announced that insurers will be responsible for paying for contraceptives, raising questions about self-insured religious groups. The ruling did not expand the religious conscience exemption to faith-based groups other than churches. Pro-life groups suggest insurance companies could raise premiums to cover the cost of contraception. The White House suggests that the policy would not allow insurers to raise premiums due to contraception.

A cross and establishment of religion

March 14, 2012: The Obama administration filed a brief with the Supreme Court in opposition to the U.S. 9th Circuit Court of Appeals' 3-0 ruling that declared a 43-foot-tall cross that serves as a war memorial on Mt. Soledad in San Diego was an unconstitutional establishment of religion. The brief states, "The decision . . . if permitted to stand, calls for the government to tear down a memorial cross that has stood for 58 years as a tribute to fallen service members. Nothing in the Establishment Clause compels that result."

Administering contraception

March 16, 2012: The Obama administration proposed further recommendations for its earlier ruling on contraception. The proposal does not expand the religious conscience exemption, specifying that the ruling would not set a precedent for future laws. The proposal suggests that a third-party administrator of the group health plan or another independent entity would assume responsibility for the contraception coverage for self-insured organizations. The final regulation will be implemented August 2013.

Religious Freedom Under Assault

Thomas S. Kidd

Thomas S. Kidd is an author and a senior fellow at Baylor University's Institute for Studies of Religion.

The next time you walk into church, or your synagogue or mosque, say a little thanks to God for our founding principles. There's a lot for which to be grateful, after all, and the freedom to worship is among our greatest blessings.

But a new report by Pew Research Center's Forum on Religion & Public Life has revealed a disturbing pattern: Nearly a third of the globe's population—2.2 billion people—live in countries where religious persecution *increased* between 2006 and 2009.

Observers have often assumed that over time, the world would progress toward what political scientist Francis Fukuyama famously called "the end of history," when Western liberal democracy would triumph over all ideological competitors. But instead, we are seeing a marked erosion of what America's Founding Fathers considered the "first freedom": the liberty of religious conscience. Even in America, there are signs that our historic commitment to this freedom is wavering.

The countries with the largest populations in the world, India and China, are among the worst offenders in social harassment or government restrictions on religion. No surprise, there. In China, the government commonly imprisons dissidents, ranging from those of the Falun Gong spiritual movement to pastors of Christian house churches. Even now, Beijing authorities are seeking to shut down the evangelical Shouwang Church, which has dared to hold outdoor assemblies.

Christians Being Targeted

In the Middle East, the "Arab Spring" has not been auspicious for religious liberty. The uprisings against repressive governments have precipitated a treacherous new era for the region's Christian minorities. According to the Pew report, Egypt was already the world's largest country with rising levels of government restrictions on religion before the ouster of Hosni Mubarak; since then, the situation has grown even worse.

Christians in the U.S. take their lumps, too, when it comes to religious freedom. These range from the frivolous . . . to real judicial infringements.

In the past six months, appalling religious violence has convulsed Egypt, especially against its Coptic Christians. Rumors about a Coptic convert to Islam being held against her will led to vicious rioting on May 8, leaving 15 dead, 200 injured, and churches looted and burned. This was only one in a series of anti-Christian incidents that has respected Middle East journalist Yasmine El Rashidi warning of an Islamist takeover in Egypt. In the Pew report, Muslim-dominated countries tended to have both high government restrictions and social pressures against religious freedom.

And what about in the USA? You won't see the kind of religious persecution here as in other parts of the world, but religious freedom is taking its hits. This is not a problem rooted exclusively in the political left or right, either.

As one might expect, some Muslims in America have faced persistent harassment since 9/11. Opponents have attempted legal measures to stop the construction of Muslim worship sites, from the controversial (and, I would argue, unnecessarily provocative) Islamic center at Ground Zero, to a neighborhood mosque in Murfreesboro, Tenn. Certain Republican leaders, such as Herman Cain, have proposed loyalty oaths for Muslims serving in government. Really. Overall, the FBI reports that more than 1,500 religious hate crimes occur annually, although the majority target Jews.

But Christians in the U.S. take their lumps, too, when it comes to religious freedom. These range from the frivolous—such as a recent (and unsuccessful) Freedom from Religion Foundation lawsuit to ban Texas Gov. Rick Perry from holding "The Response," his prayer rally in Houston—to real judicial infringements.

Freedom and the Courts

Earlier this month, for instance, a federal appeals court approved San Diego State University's policy of denying a Christian sorority and fraternity official campus benefits simply because the groups restricted membership to Christians.

And in October, the U.S. Supreme Court will hear oral arguments in what might become the most significant religious liberty case in decades, *Hosanna-Tabor Church v. EEOC*, which will, disconcertingly, consider whether a religious school has the right to fire a teacher who contradicts official church teachings.

Should the court rule against Hosanna-Tabor, it could indicate that American courts will intrude more and more upon the internal affairs of religious organizations, dictating that the right to free exercise must bow before judges' and bureaucrats' current conceptions of legal equity. Placing religious groups under special legal disadvantages, and forbidding them from operating according to their own beliefs, is certainly not what the Founders had in mind when they banned an "establishment of religion" in the First Amendment.

Let's hope that, instead, America will renew its commitment to the genius of the First Amendment's religion clauses.

The government should never promote the interests of any one faith—including secularism—but should protect the free exercise of religion for all.

In light of the Pew report, the world needs our example more than ever.

Obama's Defense of Religion

Steve Chapman

Steve Chapman is a blogger and a member of the editorial board of the Chicago Tribune.

Catholic bishops, evangelical pastors and Republican presidential candidates have been decrying the Obama administration's war on religious liberty. Amid all the uproar, it's easy to overlook something equally important: the administration's many battles *for* religious liberty.

The president has gotten deserved criticism for trying to force Catholic colleges and hospitals to buy insurance coverage for something they regard as evil: birth control. But that's only part of the story. In other realms, believers have found Barack Obama and his Justice Department to be staunch allies.

The most conspicuous surprise involves government rules for faith-based organizations that get federal funding for social services. President George W. Bush issued an executive order allowing such groups to hire only people who share their faith—exempting them from the usual ban on religious discrimination. Liberal critics accused him of underwriting "theocracy" and "faith-based coercion."

One of the opponents was Obama. In his presidential campaign, he said his view was simple: "If you get a federal grant, you can't use that grant money to proselytize to the people you help and you can't discriminate against them—or against the people you hire—on the basis of their religion."

But it hasn't worked out that way. Obama has left Bush's rule in place, infuriating many groups that expected a reversal.

They have repeatedly pressed him to bar these groups from using religious criteria in deciding whom to hire and whom to serve. Last year, the Coalition Against Religious Discrimination wrote the White House complaining that "we have seen no forward movement on this issue."

That's not the sentiment at the Institutional Religious Freedom Alliance, which includes such perennial Obama critics as the U.S. Conference of Catholic Bishops, Focus on the Family and the Southern Baptist Convention. It has taken the uncharacteristic step of siding with the administration.

"We commend your steadfast preservation of federal policies that protect the freedom of religious organizations to consider religion in making employment decisions," it informed Obama last year. "Mr. President, your appreciation for the good that religious organizations contribute on a daily basis to our society is evident."

In this instance, Obama may be accused of ignoring the establishment clause of the First Amendment, which forbids government support of religion. But if so, it's because he has given too much deference to religious freedom rather than too little.

His commitment is also on display in defending churches against municipal governments that would prefer to do without them. Under federal law, houses of worship are assured equitable treatment in land-use decisions. But mayors and community groups often tell churches to go to the devil.

When that happens, they often find themselves at odds with the Civil Rights Division of the Justice Department. Last year, it forced the town of Schodack, N.Y., to retreat after it barred an evangelical church from renting space in a commercial area where nonreligious meetings were allowed.

It filed a brief in support of a Hasidic Jewish congregation's lawsuit against the city of Los Angeles, which had forbidden it to hold services in a private home. A federal court ordered the city to back off.

The administration has also intervened in cases where prisoners are denied religious literature. After a South Carolina sheriff prohibited inmates from getting devotional materials and other publications in the mail, the Justice Department sued. In the end, the county agreed to let inmates receive Bibles, Torahs, Qurans and related fare.

In doing all this, the administration isn't simply doing the politically appealing thing. Anything but. Those who endorse letting faith-based groups have a free hand in hiring are mostly religious conservatives who wouldn't vote for Obama if he resurrected the dead.

The congregations victimized by zoning regulations are too small to matter. Prison inmates generally can't vote. There is no detectable political gain in anything Obama is doing here.

University of Virginia law professor Douglas Laycock criticized the contraceptive mandate and opposed the administration in a Supreme Court case involving a teacher fired by a religious school. But he praises its efforts to help churches and prison inmates. And on the faith-based hiring issue, he says, Obama has actually been "kind of heroic."

The president's detractors may continue to portray him as a secular fanatic with, as Rick Santorum claims, an "overt hostility to faith in America." Before they do, though, they might want to remember the Ten Commandments—especially the one about bearing false witness.

Protecting Access to Birth Control Does Not Violate Religious Freedom

Robert Creamer

Robert Creamer is an author; a political organizer and strategist; a partner in Democracy Partners, a training organization for political organizers; and a senior strategist for Americans United for Change, a liberal policy group.

In many respects it is amazing that in 2012 there is a controversy over women's access to birth control.

Let's be clear, the current controversy over the [Barack] Obama administration's rules that require all employers who provide health insurance to provide birth control without a co-pay to its women employees, has nothing whatsoever to do with religious freedom.

It has everything to do with an attempt to take away women's access to easy, affordable birth control, no matter where they work.

Birth control is not controversial. Surveys show that 99 percent of women and 98 percent of Catholic women have used birth control at some time in their lives.

No one is trying to require that anyone else use birth control if it violates their religious convictions. But the convictions of some religious leaders should not be allowed to trump the rights of women employees to have access to birth control.

The Contraceptive Rule

The rule in question exempts 355,000 churches from this requirement since they presumably hire individuals who share the religious faith of the institutions in question. But it does not exempt universities and hospitals that may be owned by religious organizations, but serve—and employ—people of all faiths to engage in decidedly secular activities. These are not "religious institutions." They are engaged in the normal flow of commerce, even though they are owned by religious organizations.

The overwhelming majority of Americans oppose taking away the ability for women to have easy, affordable access to birth control.

Some religious leaders argue that they should not be required to pay for birth control coverage for their employees if they have religious objections to birth control. This argument ignores the fact that health insurance coverage is not a voluntary gift to employees. It is a part of their compensation package. If someone opposed the minimum wage on religious grounds—say because they believed it "discouraged individual initiative"—that wouldn't excuse them from having to pay the minimum wage.

If a Christian Science institution opposed invasive medical treatment on religious grounds, it would not be allowed to provide health care plans that fund only spiritual healing.

Many Americans opposed the Iraq War—some on religious grounds. That did not excuse them from paying taxes to the government.

Support for Contraception

The overwhelming majority of Americans oppose taking away the ability for women to have easy, affordable access to birth control. A Public Policy Polling survey released yesterday [February 7, 2012] found that 56 percent of voters support the decision to require health plans to cover prescription birth control with no additional out-of-pocket fees, while only 37 percent opposed. Fifty-three percent of Catholic voters favor the benefit.

Fifty-seven percent of voters think that women employed by Catholic hospitals and universities should have the same rights to contraceptive coverage as other women.

No doubt these numbers would be vastly higher if the poll were limited to the employees of those hospitals and universities because eliminating the requirement of coverage would cost the average woman $600 to $1,200 per year in out-of-pocket costs.

Twenty-eight states already require organizations that offer prescription insurance to cover contraception.

But ironically, requiring birth control coverage generally costs nothing to the institution that provides it. That's because by making birth control accessible, health plans cut down on the number of unwanted pregnancies that cost a great deal more. And of course they also cut down on the number of abortions.

That may help explain why many Catholic-owned universities already provide coverage for birth control. For instance, a Georgetown University spokesperson told *ThinkProgress* yesterday that employees "have access to health insurance plans offered and designed by national providers to a national pool. These plans include coverage for birth control."

The University of San Francisco, the University of Scranton, DePaul University in Chicago, Boston College—all have health insurance plans that cover contraception.

And, finally, this is nothing new. Twenty-eight states already require organizations that offer prescription insurance to cover contraception.

The Population Problem

Of course the shocking thing about this entire controversy is that there is a worldwide consensus that the use of birth control is one of society's most important moral priorities. Far from being something that should be discouraged, or is controversial, the use of birth control is critical to the survival and success of humanity.

In 1968, the world's population reached 3.5 billion people. On October 31, 2011, the *United Nations Population Division* reported that the world population had reached seven billion. It had *doubled* in 43 years.

It took 90,000 years of human development for the population to reach 1 billion. Over the last two centuries the population has grown by another six billion.

In fact, in the first 12 years of the 21st Century, we have already added a billion people to the planet.

It is simply not possible for this small planet to sustain that kind of exponential human population growth. If we do, the result will be poverty, war, the depletion of our natural resources and famine. Fundamentally, the Reverend Malthus was right—except that the result is not inevitable.

Population growth is not something that just happens to us. We can choose whether or not to reproduce and at what rates.

No force is required. The evidence shows that the population explosion stops where there is the availability of birth control and women have educational opportunity.

That's why it is our *moral imperative* to act responsibly and encourage each other to use birth control. And it's not a hard sell. Children are the greatest blessing you can have in life. But most people are eager to limit the number of children they have if they have access to contraception. We owe it to those children—to the next generation and the generation after that—to act responsibly and stabilize the size of the human population.

The moral thing to do is to make certain that every woman who wants it has access to birth control.

Catholic Bishops Want to Deny Women the Religious Freedom to Choose Contraception

Jessica Coblentz

Jessica Coblentz is a Catholic writer and a PhD student in theology at Boston College.

When the U.S. Conference of Catholic Bishops [USCCB] kicked off their "Fortnight for Freedom" campaign almost two weeks ago [June 21, 2012], they chose an auspicious feast day to start. On the Church's liturgical calendar, June 21 commemorates two martyrs who suffered political persecution: St. Thomas More and St. John Fisher, who were killed under Henry VIII for refusing to recognize him as the head of the Church of England. The American bishops have indicated they feel similarly besieged by political forces. To promote "our Christian and American heritage of liberty," they've organized two weeks of activism and prayer, culminating in a nationally televised liturgy on July 4, Independence Day—another date with clear significance for this U.S.-focused event.

At the forefront of the bishops' crusade is, of course, their opposition to the Obama administration's health insurance mandate requiring institutions—including many Catholic ones—to provide contraception coverage. Though the administration has tried to widen the mandate's exemptions, the USCCB argues that because Catholic doctrine does not condone contraception, the mandate constitutes a violation of religious liberty. The USCCB and its rallying cry have called the largest U.S. religious body, totaling more than 65 million members, into action. From Allentown, Pennsylvania, to Youngstown, Ohio, parishes and dioceses are hosting Fortnight for Freedom events, tolling church bells to "mark our gratitude for our First Freedom," praying the "Patriotic Rosary," and contacting Congress to voice their opposition to the mandate. The bishops are urging church members to text "FREEDOM" to join the campaign, and using church bulletin inserts to tell parishioners, "We cannot remain silent."

American Catholicism has a history of extolling the virtues of individual religious freedoms—even when it contradicts official Church teachings.

Denying Religious Freedom to Pro-Conception Catholic Women

Likewise, critics of the campaign refuse to remain silent. In the reaction against Fortnight for Freedom, some are responding to the bishops on their own terms. If the campaign is about religious liberty, they ask, then whose liberty is at stake? The bishops present the Catholic exercise of religious liberty as the ability to *reject* the use of contraception, or at least the financing of insurance plans that cover contraceptive services. The irony, to those on the other side, is that a campaign meant to promote religious liberty actually *denies* the religious freedom of many Catholic women, who rely on their personal religious convictions to determine their stance on contraception and the mandate. Studies show that as many as 98 percent of sexually experienced American Catholic women over the age of 18 have used contraception. A recent PRRI/RNS [Public Religion Research Institute/Religion News Service] poll reports that a majority of American Catholics do not see the contraception mandate as a threat to religious freedom, indicating that many hold a broader understanding of religious liberty than the bishops maintain. The debate surrounding the mandate, then, is not only about contraception and religious liberty. It is also about who gets to define religious liberty's very meaning.

Catholics for Choice (CFC), a reproductive rights group, has orchestrated the most expansive effort to actively engage the USCCB argument about religious liberty. In a statement, CFC asks the question, "Whose religious freedom are we talking about?" They argue, "No-cost contraception for the average woman, including many Catholic women, can mean following her religious beliefs, following her conscience." Likewise, parishioners at The Shrine of the Most Blessed Sacrament parish in Washington D.C. released a public statement criticizing the campaign's narrow depiction of religious liberty. "We, the faithful, are in danger of becoming pawns," they stated. "In no way do we feel that our religious freedom is at risk. We find it grotesque to have the call for this 'Fortnight' evoke the names of holy martyrs who died resisting tyranny." Other Catholics, from the editors of *Commonweal Magazine* to Bishop Stephen Blaire of Stockton, California, have criticized the shortsighted, partisan nature of the USCCB's charge that the mandate poses a threat to religious freedom.

So long as the all-male Catholic clergy solely possess the authority to identify what does and does not constitute a free, religiously-motivated choice worthy of legal protection, women have no official authority in Catholic religious liberty conversations whatsoever.

A Contentious Issue

Religious liberty has long been an important yet contentious issue for Catholics. The faith's status as a minority sect throughout much of American history set its members apart from other religious adherents and afforded a unique role in legal debates about religious freedom. Early court cases regarding Catholic parochial schools, for instance, were influential milestones in the development of church and state relations. But even as Catholics have long sought protection under religious liberty, they have not always been in agreement about it. Disagreement has often stemmed from the fact that American Catholicism has a history of extolling the virtues of individual religious freedoms—even when it contradicts official Church teachings.

In 1960, Jesuit John Courtney Murray—one of American Catholicism's most influential theologians on religious freedom—published his most famous book, *We Hold These Truths: Catholic Reflections on the American Proposition*, where he articulated the compatibility of Catholicism and American thought, particularly the First Amendment. Murray then went on to serve as a theological advisor during Vatican II, where he greatly influenced the Council's 1965 statement on religious freedom, *Dignitatis Humanae* (*DH*), which said an individual's conscience mediates "the imperatives of divine law." Consequently, one "is not to be forced to act in manner contrary to his conscience. Nor, on the other hand, is he to be restrained from acting in accordance with his conscience, especially in matters religious." The document assigned the responsibility of protecting religious liberty both to the state and to religious groups. Marking a turning point in Catholic teaching, it declared support for the constitutional protection of religious liberty—a stark contrast from the days of Christendom. The complementary limitations of church and state protected an individual's ability to act according to his or her conscience, especially concerning religious matters.

With the appearance of oral contraceptives in the early 1960s, little time passed before Catholics brought Vatican II's declarations on religious liberty to bear on contraception. In a memo to Boston's Richard Cardinal Cushing after Massachusetts decriminalized artificial contraception, John Courtney

Murray argued that contraception is a matter of private morality and thus one that ought to be protected by Catholics under religious liberty. When Pope Paul VI reaffirmed the Church's doctrinal stance against contraception in the 1968 papal letter *Humanae Vitae*, there was a public outcry from North American Catholics who opposed the letter on the grounds of religious liberty. In the United States, Catholic University's Charles Curran mobilized 600 theologians for a press conference where they announced their opposition to *Humanae Vitae*, arguing that dissent from the Vatican's position on contraception was permissible when discerned responsibly and for the sake of one's marriage. The Canadian Council of Catholic Bishops issued the Winnipeg Statement that year, asserting that any Catholic who "honestly chooses that course which seems right to him does so in good conscience," echoing the language of *Dignitatis Humanae*. Citing the "accepted principles of moral theology," the bishops argued that an act in good conscience is moral even if one acts against the Vatican's doctrinal teaching on contraception.

The Catholic theological tradition insists that religious liberty ought to protect the ability of a woman to obey her conscience.

Female Catholics' Choices and Religious Liberty

Critics of the bishops' current battle can call on this Catholic history of religious liberty and individual freedom. In their view, women's choices are an issue of religious liberty—not merely a threat to it. Still, who defines religious liberty remains a matter of authority—and a highly gendered one at that. When the USCCB conveys that the rejection of contraception is the only religiously-motivated choice that warrants the protection of religious liberty among Catholics, they assert the message that only church leaders have the authority to determine what counts as religious behavior. This strips other Catholics of the legitimate authority to negotiate their tradition when determining their own religiously-motivated actions. What is more, so long as the all-male Catholic clergy solely possess the authority to identify what does and does not constitute a free, religiously-motivated choice worthy of legal protection, women have no official authority in Catholic religious liberty conversations whatsoever. As it stands, the religious decisions and actions of all Catholics other than clergy—be they *for or against* contraception and contraceptive coverage—are seemingly insignificant in "Catholic" concerns about religious liberty.

The public rhetoric surrounding the HHS mandate has only reified the debates' gender lines. As [author] Michael Sean Winters observed earlier this year, the bishops are framing the mandate debate in terms of religious liberty in opposition to those who frame the discussion in terms of women's rights. A series of events in February bolstered the position of those advocating for a women's rights perspective—namely the absence of women at the official congressional hearing concerning the mandate and Rush Limbaugh's "slut" fiasco that arose in response to Sandra Fluke's testimony during an unofficial Democrat-sponsored hearing. The Fortnight for Freedom campaign can be viewed as an attempt to reemphasize the religious liberty stakes in the debate.

Yet the mandate is not simply a "women's issue" because it concerns contraception; the mandate is a "women's issue" because it concerns religious liberty, as the bishops insist, and the Catholic theological tradition insists that religious liberty ought to protect the ability of a woman to obey her conscience. The bishops, or anyone for that matter, need not theologically condone the contraceptive decisions of Catholic women in order to recognize them as exercises of free, religious choice. Yet the current rhetoric of the USCCB's "Fortnight for Freedom" campaign does not. With last week's Supreme Court decision to uphold the Affordable Care Act that contains the HHS contraception mandate, the USCCB has vowed to continue its opposition campaign. But if the bishops continue to exclude so many American Catholics from their representation of religious liberty—notably, the majority of Catholic Women—the USCCB fails in its own stated aim to protect the religious liberty of all.

Current
CONTROVERSIES

CHAPTER 3

What Role Does Religion Play in International Politics?

Chapter Preface

Religion has long played a role in US foreign policy, but in 1998 the US Congress passed a law mandating that the president, the State Department, and the Congress promote religious liberty as a key part of US relations with other countries. The International Religious Freedom Act (IRFA) was signed into law by President Bill Clinton on October 27, 1998. Its overall goal is to convince other countries, including newly emerging democracies, that freedom of religion is a fundamental human right that must be honored in order to create national and global stability. The act gives the US president various options in responding to countries that commit or permit particularly egregious acts of religious persecution or violations of religious freedom. However, the IRFA also permits the president to waive sanctions against a particular country—an option that sometimes undermines the nation's commitment to religious freedom in favor of other national security priorities.

The IRFA came about because of congressional awareness of the growing pattern of religious persecution around the world. Many governments sanction one particular religion as the state religion and either openly tolerate religious persecution against minority faiths or take actions to restrict or otherwise interfere with the practices of other religions. Examples cited to support the legislation included Russia's religious restrictions; China's repression of Catholics and Protestant Christians, Buddhists in Tibet, and other religions; and Sudan's civil war, which was waged, in part, because of religious differences between ruling Muslims in the northern part of the country and Christians and other non-Muslims who mostly live in the south.

The IRFA obligates the Congress and the president to consider religious freedom issues when formulating US foreign policies. The president is required to identify specific countries that severely violate religious freedom—called countries of particular concern (CPC)—and then work with officials in the State Department and other foreign policy experts to respond to those countries. Title IV of the IFRA lists the options available in designing the US response. These include: a demarche (diplomatic message or protest); a public or private condemnation; cancellation, denial, or delay of cultural or scientific exchanges; cancellation, denial, or delay of state visits; withholding of humanitarian or other forms of US or international aid; and sanctions prohibiting the US government from entering into import or export agreements with the offending nation. Although the original legislation mandated sanctions against serious violators of religious freedom, the IFRA was amended before final passage to give the president the flexibility to refrain from taking punitive actions against a country shown to be violating religious freedom, in order to achieve other important US foreign policy or security interests.

The act sets up a structure for implementing its provisions, including the establishment of the Office of the International Religious Freedom at the US Department of State, which is led by an ambassador at large for international religious freedom. This office advises the president and the State Department on religious freedom issues and is responsible for publishing an annual report on international religious freedom (IRFR). This document describes the state of religious freedom existing in each country and explains what the United States is doing to respond to violators. The act also sets up a commission on international religious freedom (USCIRF) and a special advisor to the president on international religious freedom within the National Security Council. The commission is a body of experts, including the ambassador at large, that reviews annual reports and makes foreign policy recommendations to the president.

The passage of the IRFA made the United States unusual as one of the few countries in the world that promotes religious freedom openly as part of its foreign policy. Whether the act has achieved its goal of expanding religious freedom, however, is a matter of debate. Some observers note that the act has been helpful in publicizing the problem of religious persecution. The annual report on international religious freedom, in particular, is a resource used throughout the world to measure the degree to which religious freedom is being curtailed or threatened. However, critics argue that human rights, including religious freedom, continue to play only a small role in US foreign policy. They point out that the United States often grants waivers to countries known to be violators of religious freedom and in many other cases chooses weak sanctions against violators. Other critics assert that little has been done to advance the cause of religious freedom. For example, critics say the United States has failed to engage Islamic actors in Egypt, where the Arab Spring uprisings have produced an Islamist government. Still other critics argue that the United States has no right to push American ideas about religious freedom on other cultures that do not embrace this value. The authors of viewpoints included in this chapter address the basic question of whether religion is having an undue influence on international politics.

Religious Persecution Is Widespread Around the World

Andy Bannister

Andy Bannister is the Canadian director for Ravi Zacharias International Ministries (RZIM) Canada, a global team of speakers and writers who address issues related to faith, culture, politics, and society.

Dr. John Joseph was the Catholic Bishop of Faisalabad in Pakistan and a prominent human rights activist. On 6 May 1998, he travelled from his home to the city of Sahiwal to address a prayer meeting being held for victims of blasphemy cases. In Pakistan, the notorious 295-C law makes insulting Muhammad or the Qur'an [also called the Koran, the Islamic holy book] a crime punishable by death. The law is often used to falsely accuse religious minorities, especially Christians, and Dr. Joseph was concerned about one Christian in particular, Ayub Masih. Arrested in 1996 for allegedly violating the blasphemy laws, Ayub Masih had been held in solitary confinement in a tiny cell, denied medical care, and frequently abused. In April 1998, he had been formally found guilty and had been sentenced to death. After addressing the prayer meeting, Dr. Joseph made his way to the courthouse to the spot where, during the trial, somebody had shot at Ayub Masih and tried to assassinate him. At about 9:30 pm, Dr. Joseph took a pistol and took his own life. In a letter to a local newspaper, published after his death, he had written: "dedicated persons do not count the cost of the sacrifices they have to make".

Andy Bannister, "The Causes and Roots of Religious Persecution—Part 1," *The Bayview Review*, January 9, 2012. Copyright © 2012 by The Bayview Review. All rights reserved. Reproduced by permission.

Bishop John Joseph wanted to draw attention to the dire situation facing Pakistan's two million Christians. Everything else had been tried, but the international community seemed deaf to their plight. Frustrated, he concluded that only something so dramatic as his taking his own life would effect any change.

Sadly, it seems that his hope was misplaced. Although the international community is now more aware than ever of religious persecution, the situation is still bleak. It is presently estimated that some 200 million Christians in 60 countries live under daily threat of persecution. Between 2008 and 2009, 176,000 were killed. Some estimate that if nothing is done, then by 2025, an average of 210,000 Christians will be being killed each year.

Today, religious persecution occurs around the world in a wide variety of countries and contexts.

Just last week [January 2, 2012], the Catholic charity, Aid to the Church in Need, launched its annual report on religious freedom worldwide. It concluded that 75% of all religious persecution in the world is currently directed at Christian minorities. Archbishop Warda of Erbil in Iraq spoke about the difficulties in his country and commented:

> We wonder if we will survive as a people in our own country. . . . The past is terrifying, the present is not promising.

Persecution is such a regular occurrence that it comes as no surprise that more than half the Christians in Iraq have fled. A community once numbering over a million is now down to about 150,000. Canon Andrew White who runs St. George's Anglican Church in Baghdad and is internationally known for his work on human rights and peace making, put it bluntly in an interview with CBS. Noting that the congregation at St. George's were mainly women and children the interviewer asked, "where are the men?" White replied: "They are mainly killed. Some are kidnapped. Some are killed. Here in this church, all of my original leadership were taken and killed."

How can it be, in the twenty-first century, that hundreds of millions of people are living in fear and are not free to worship or express their religious beliefs in safety?

Religious Persecution: A Global Tragedy

Religious persecution doesn't just effect Christians. In the last two millennia, some 200 million people have been killed because of their religious affiliation; those rates are not improving. Today, religious persecution occurs around the world in a wide variety of countries and contexts. One group who have also suffered tremendously are the Ahmadiyah Muslim sect. Considered heretical by mainstream Islam, the Ahmadiyah are banned and persecuted in many Muslim countries. For example, in Indonesia, the government passed a decree in 2008 requiring Ahmadiyah Muslims to "stop spreading interpretations and activities that deviate from the principal teachings of Islam". Those kind of signals from the government simply encourage extremist groups. Thus it was on 1 February 2011 that a mob of 1,500 men attacked twenty Ahmadiyah members in a village in Western Java. They broke into the house where the group was meeting, ordered the men to strip naked, then videoed them being beaten with sticks, hoes and machetes, before torching the building. Three died and six were wounded.

We could easily fill an entire library with such tragic stories. As Asma Jahangir, the UN Special Rapporteur on Religious Freedom or Belief wrote:

[Discrimination] based on religion or belief preventing individuals from fully enjoying all their human rights still occurs worldwide on a daily basis.

Where Is Persecution Happening?

All of this is deeply troubling. As with most human rights abuses, it's hard to discuss these things dispassionately: lives are broken, damaged and destroyed on a daily basis. But why is this happening? How can it be, in the twenty-first century, that hundreds of millions of people are living in fear and are not free to worship or express their religious beliefs in safety? Can we identify any patterns to religious persecution across the globe, any causes or trends that might help us formulate a response?

The answer to that question is yes. But let's begin by taking a step back and asking where precisely it is that religious persecution is happening. Whilst persecution is a global phenomena, there are patterns that we can track.

Brian Grim and Roger Finke, two sociologists who have produced some of the most recent analyses of religious persecution, have used a number of studies to answer this very question: where is persecution happening. Their figures look like this: [Muslim Majority 62%, Other Majority (Atheist, Buddhist, Hindu, Jewish) 85%, No Religion 33%, Christian Majority 28%, and World Average 43%.]

If we look at even higher rates of persecution, the differences are also striking:

> Persecution of more than one thousand persons is present in 45 percent of Muslim-majority countries and 60 percent of the "Other Majority" religion countries, compared to 11 percent of Christian-majority countries and 8 percent of countries where no single religion holds a majority.

These figures are consistently backed up by other studies. For example, Open Doors, a well-respected Christian agency that lobbies on behalf of persecuted Christians, publishes an annual "World Watch List". Their 2011 report listed 51 countries of concern: 65% were Muslim-majority countries. Of the top ten human rights offenders, seven were Muslim-majority and two were communist atheistic states.

What could be the cause of these kind of figures? As Grim and Finke dig deeper and compare statistics from a wide range of countries, they quickly draw a conclusion. The common denominator, the common link—whether the country in which the persecution is occurring is Muslim or atheist, Hindu, Buddhist, or no-majority-religion—is religious regulation. There is a direct correlation between attempts by a state to control, regulate or restrict religious activity and religious persecution. Restriction on or regulation of religion is a surprisingly common phenomena. According to the Pew Forum:

> [N]early 70 percent of the world's 6.8 billion people live in countries with high restrictions on religion, the brunt of which often falls on religious minorities.

Social pressures and state pressures on religious freedom often work together.

There are two ways that a state can attempt to control religious activity or restrict religious freedom within its borders. First, a government can use the full force of the state, for example by passing laws, arresting or harassing worshippers or religious leaders. So, for example, in China, the communist government has just marked the start of the Christian season of Lent by bulldozing churches and rounding up Christians, something it does every year, to remind them of the consequences of daring to be a religious believer in the officially atheistic People's Republic.

As well as using all the apparatus of the state, a government can also encourage or allow social pressure build up to make it hard for the members of a minority religious community to practice their faith. For example, in 2006 an Afghan man, Abdul Rahman, was arrested for apostasy [abandonment of religion]. The Afghan government, cognisant of the negative publicity the story was gaining as it spread around the world, were minded to release him. Senior Islamic clerics got wind of this and warned that they would incite people to kill him unless he reverted to Islam. When Abdul Rahman was released, three days later, hundreds of clerics and students marched in the streets crying "Death to Christians!"

Social pressures and state pressures on religious freedom often work together, mutually reinforcing one another. A tragic example of this occurred in Pakistan this year. On 4 January [2012], the governor of Punjab province, Salman Taseer, was getting into his car at a market when one of his own bodyguards opened fire and shot him 26 times. Why? The bodyguard was angry that Mr. Taseer was opposed to Pakistan's blasphemy law and had appealed for the pardon of a Christian woman, Asia Bibi, who had been sentenced to death for allegedly insulting Muhammad. A few months later, another politician, Shahbaz Bhatti, the Minority Affairs Minister and the only Christian in Pakistan's cabinet, was gunned down, again because of his well-publicised opposition to the blasphemy laws.

Those tragic stories illustrate the way that social pressures and government pressures on religious minorities work together and cause persecution. If the Pakistan government had the courage to remove the 295-C blasphemy law, this would remove much of the fuel from the fire that popular Islamist movements are trying to light.

How Do You Solve a Problem Like *Sharia*?

This connection between social restrictions, government restrictions and violent religious persecution also help to illuminate a phenomena we saw earlier: the extremely high rate of religious persecution in Muslim-majority countries. As

Brian Grim and Roger Finke put it:

> Religious persecution is not only more prevalent among Muslim-majority countries, but it also generally occurs at more severe levels.

The problem is simply this. Built into Islam is a ready-made system of religious law, *Sharia*. Because a whole codified body of religious law is readily available, governments in Muslim-majority countries face an ever present temptation to draw upon or incorporate aspects of *Sharia* into their legal systems. Unlike many Western bodies of law, *Sharia* is far more wide-ranging and includes regulations that encompass morality and religion and many of its stipulations have implications for religious minorities.

Many Muslim countries have incorporated *Sharia* law, or aspects of it into their legal system and constitutions. Those that haven't face a growing popular pressure to do so. A 2006 Gallup survey of ten Muslim-majority countries found that 79% wanted *Sharia* in some form. Indeed, 66% of Egyptians and 60% of Pakistanis said they wanted *Sharia* as the only source of legislation. Even an astonishing 40% of British Muslims said they wanted *Sharia*.

When it comes to religious persecution, it is vital to stress that the problem is not Muslims. *The problem is* Sharia.

The implementation of *Sharia* law is directly connected to the problems of religious freedom and religious persecution in Muslim-majority countries, the states where persecution rates are among the highest in the world. But here we enter a very difficult area of discussion. When it comes to talking about Islam and these kind of issues, there are two traps one can fall into. One is to be overly critical, lumping all Muslims together as a group, not appreciating the wide diversity and ranges of opinion within the world's 1.6 billion Muslims. But if being

95

overly critical is one error, the other is to be overly timid and to not ask any difficult questions or to raise any controversial issues.

How can we best navigate between these two pitfalls? I have been researching, teaching and writing on Islam for fifteen years now and do so unapologetically as a Christian. For me, I've found an observation made by Anglican vicar and human rights activist, Mark Durie, very helpful. Mark speaks of the need to hold two things together—love and respect for the other but also truth. He writes:

> Love for the other and truth are two attributes to be held together, the one complementing the other. Truth without love can be harsh and even cruel, but love without truth can be equally as dangerous as, lacking discernment, it steers the soul into shipwreck after shipwreck.

We also need to be willing to recognise something that's often neglected in these discussions. The importance of different worldviews. Just as different political ideologies can produce vastly different societies, even next door to one another—compare communist North with capitalist South Korea—so different religious worldviews exert very different influences. The Qur'an does not produce the same kinds of societies as the Judeo-Christian worldview whilst Buddhist, Hinduism or Marxist-Atheism produce different results again.

But when it comes to religious persecution, it is vital to stress that the problem is not *Muslims*. The problem is *Sharia*. To misquote Rogers and Hammerstein: how do you solve a problem like *Sharia*?

Islam Has Emerged as a Political Force in the Middle East

Michael A. Lange

Michael A. Lange is head of the political dialogue and analysis team at the Department for European and International Cooperation of Konrad-Adenauer-Stiftung, a political party foundation in Berlin, Germany.

Following the election of the Ennahda Party in Tunisia in October 2011 and the Justice and Development Party (PJD) in Morocco in November 2011, the decisive victory by the Muslim Brotherhood's Freedom and Justice Party (FJP) in the parliamentary elections in Egypt at the turn of the year 2011/2012 seemed to confirm an Islamic trend: the Arab Spring has since led to a conspicuous "Islamic awakening".

A Continuing Islamic Trend

Forthcoming elections in Algeria and Libya, as well as planned elections in Yemen and the Palestinian Autonomous Area are already looming. There is much evidence to suggest that this Islamic trend will continue. Without free elections by secret ballot, it is not possible to install those requisite democratically legitimate constitutional bodies that are called upon to exert a determining influence on the future political order of their countries. All elections, whether they are for short-term constituent assemblies or for representative bodies elected for full legislative periods, will have a decisive influence not only on the soon to be relevant party political spectrum, but also on the political balance of power in the various Arab states that are currently undergoing comprehensive political transformation.

Egypt, the Arab country with the largest population and therefore traditionally the most influential, will have a particularly important role to play in this regional transition process. If political transition is successful in Egypt, then it is possible that the process of democratic change in the Arab world will continue and conceivably prevail. If transition is seen to fail there early on, then it will also be more difficult for other countries in the region to bring their own transition processes to a successful conclusion. Egypt, which has a comparatively heterogeneous population, will be a decisive test case, not only for the future relationship between Islam-inspired and secular political movements, but also for relations between ultra-orthodox and liberal forms of Islam. Additionally, the expected re-positioning of the Egyptian military within a new constitutional system will be a significant challenge in itself, and it will no doubt have an influence on similar security sector reform processes in neighbouring Arab countries.

[The] sum of imponderables will not only continue to encumber the transition process in Egypt, but also preoccupy the entire region for a long time to come.

What are the likely ramifications for politics, the economy and society of policies that will influence the government's future work, if the policies are more clearly oriented towards the implementation of Islamic Sharia law? What rights and how much tolerance will religious and secular minorities receive in a new political order of this kind, without inciting a cultural war? How will the new Islamic parties create the kind of economic new beginning that is needed without coming into conflict with the restrictive tenets of Islam, and what stance should European countries, especially Germany, take towards these election victors with their Islamic leanings? Will future political dialogue with governments determined by Islamic powers in North African countries that are undergoing transition continue to be characterized by the kind of scepticism EU [European Union] countries displayed in reaction to the 2006 election victory of Hamas (basically another offshoot of the Muslim Brotherhood, who were victorious in Egypt), or will the practicalities of *Realpolitik* call for a re-evaluation? All these questions need to be considered when viewing the political upheavals that will be related to significant electoral victories for political Islam in North Africa.

Transition Concepts: Road Maps for Change

The demands of the "rebellious youth" in Tunisia and Egypt, as well as other autocratic states such as Libya and Syria, for more human rights and social justice, as part of a comprehensive restructuring of the existing political order, won the almost wholehearted support of political observers in Europe from the onset. However, in recent months these demands have taken the various countries down some very different paths. Since the power structures that were firmly established only a few months ago have not yet demonstrated the necessary willingness to introduce the kind of reforms that are needed to lead their countries out of the political cul-de-sac of unresolved succession issues and unsatisfactory political and economic reform processes, a different kind of change to the political order has been set in motion, which will undoubtedly be even more challenging, in as much as the potential political ramifications of such a change are far more difficult to assess. It is important not only to structure these changes in a coherent manner, but to do so in as peaceful a way as possible, so that the changes lead to an outcome that is acceptable to all concerned. This has been and continues to be no easy task.

The individual countries in North Africa have since chosen entirely different paths on the way to a new political order. The transition processes in the various countries differ not only in terms of protagonists, but also in terms of the intensity of the accompanying resistance and protests. Following the removal or expulsion of their former autocratic leaders, each of the countries initially had to deal with the issue of what to do with the "remains of the ruling political class", who had close ties to former autocratic regimes. This sum of imponderables will not only continue to encumber the transition process in Egypt, but also preoccupy the entire region for a long time to come. It will certainly be some time before the people of these countries are able to return to their familiar, not particularly political, everyday lives. Awaiting subsidence of the current tumultuous political situation will require much patience from the citizens of these countries. There are many good reasons for Europe in particular to hope that they will find this patience. If they do not, it seems unlikely that the current transition process will be brought to a successful conclusion, with all the attendant unpleasant consequences for political dialogue and economic cooperation with the countries of North Africa.

Fear the Muslim Brotherhood

Andrew C. McCarthy

Andrew C. McCarthy is an author and a senior fellow at the National Review Institute, a conservative public policy and advocacy organization.

At the *Daily Beast*, Bruce Riedel has posted an essay called "Don't fear Egypt's Muslim Brotherhood," the classic, conventional-wisdom response to the crisis in Egypt. The Muslim Brotherhood is just fine, he'd have you believe, no need to worry. After all, the Brothers have even renounced violence!

One might wonder how an organization can be thought to have renounced violence when it has inspired more jihadists than any other, and when its Palestinian branch, the Islamic Resistance Movement, is probably more familiar to you by the name Hamas—a terrorist organization committed by charter to the violent destruction of Israel. Indeed, in recent years, the Brotherhood (a.k.a., the Ikhwan) has enthusiastically praised jihad and even applauded—albeit in more muted tones—Osama bin Laden. None of that, though, is an obstacle for Mr. Riedel, a former CIA officer who is now a Brookings scholar and Obama administration national-security adviser. Following the template the progressive (and bipartisan) foreign-policy establishment has been sculpting for years, his "no worries" conclusion is woven from a laughably incomplete history of the Ikhwan.

By his account, Brotherhood founder Hassan al-Banna "preached a fundamentalist Islamism and advocated the creation of an Islamic Egypt, but he was also open to importing techniques of political organization and propaganda from Europe that rapidly made the Brotherhood a fixture in Egyptian politics." What this omits, as I recount in *The Grand Jihad*, is that terrorism and paramilitary training were core parts of Banna's program. It is by leveraging the resulting atmosphere of intimidation that the Brotherhood's "politics" have achieved success. The Ikhwan's activist organizations follow the same program in the United States, where they enjoy outsize political influence because of the terrorist onslaught.

Banna was a practical revolutionary. On the one hand, he instructed his votaries to prepare for violence. They had to understand that, in the end—when the time was right, when the Brotherhood was finally strong enough that violent attacks would more likely achieve Ikhwan objectives than provoke crippling blowback—violence would surely be necessary to complete the revolution (meaning, to institute sharia, Islam's legal-political framework). Meanwhile, on the other hand, he taught that the Brothers should take whatever they could get from the regime, the political system, the legal system, and the culture. He shrewdly realized that, if the Brothers did not overplay their hand, if they duped the media, the intelligentsia, and the public into seeing them as fighters for social justice, these institutions would be apt to make substantial concessions. Appeasement, he knew, is often a society's first response to a threat it does not wish to believe is existential.

Here's Riedel again:

> By World War 2, [the Brotherhood] became more violent in its opposition to the British and the British-dominated monarchy, sponsoring assassinations and mass violence. After the army seized power in 1952, [the Brotherhood] briefly flirted with supporting Gamal Abdel Nasser's government but then moved into opposition. Nasser ruthlessly suppressed it.

This history is selective to the point of parody. The Brotherhood did not suddenly become violent (or "more violent") during World War II. It was violent from its origins two decades earlier. This fact—along with Egyptian Islamic society's deep antipathy toward the West and its attraction to the Nazis' virulent anti-Semitism—is what gradually beat European powers, especially Britain, into withdrawal.

Banna himself was killed in 1949, during the Brotherhood's revolt against the British-backed monarchy. Thereafter, the Brotherhood did not wait until after the Free Officers Movement seized power to flirt with Nasser. They were part of the coup, Nasser having personally lobbied Sayyid Qutb (the most significant Ikhwan figure after Banna's death) for an alliance.

Omitting this detail helps Riedel whitewash the Brothers' complicity in what befell them. The Ikhwan did not seamlessly "move into the opposition" once Nasser came to power. First, it deemed itself double-crossed by Nasser, who had wooed the Brotherhood into the coup by signaling sympathy for its Islamist agenda but then, once in power, declined to implement elements of sharia. Furthermore, Nasser did not just wake up one day and begin "ruthlessly suppressing" the Brotherhood; the Ikhwan tried to assassinate him. It was at that point, when the Islamist coup attempt against the new regime failed, that the strongman cracked down relentlessly.

Riedel next asserts: "Nasser and his successors, Anwar Sadat and Mubarak, have alternatively repressed and demonized the Brotherhood or tolerated it as an anti-communist and right-wing opposition." This, too, is hopelessly wrong and incomplete. To begin with, regardless of how obdurately progressives repeat the claim, Islamism is not a right-wing movement. The Brotherhood's is a revolutionary program, the political and economic components of which are essentially socialist. It is no accident that Islamists in America are among the staunchest supporters of Obamacare and other redistributionist elements of the Obama agenda. In his *Social Justice in Islam*, Qutb concludes that Marx's system is far superior to capitalism, which Islamists deplore. Communism, he argues, faltered principally in its rigid economic determinism, thus missing the spiritual components of Allah's totalitarian plan—

though Qutb compared it favorably to Christianity, which he saw as insufficiently attentive to earthly concerns.

Nasser's persecution of the Ikhwan led many of its leading figures to flee Egypt for Saudi Arabia, where the Brothers were welcomed because they were perceived, quite correctly, as urbane but stalwart jihadists who would greatly benefit a backwards society—especially its education system (Banna and Qutb were both academics, and the Brotherhood teemed with professionals trained in many disciplines). The toxic mix of Saudi billions and Brotherhood ideology—the marriage of Saudi Wahhabism and Brotherhood Salafism—created the modern Islamist movement and inspired many of the terrorist organizations (including al-Qaeda) and other Islamist agitators by which we are confronted today. That Wahhabism and Salafism are fundamentalist doctrines does not make them right-wing. In fact, Islamism is in a virulent historical phase, and is a far more daunting challenge to the West than it was a half-century ago, precisely because its lavishly funded extremism has overwhelmed the conservative constraints of Arab culture.

The Brotherhood seems comparatively moderate, if only because the most horrific atrocities have been committed by two even worse terrorist organizations.

Sadat pivoted away from his predecessor's immersion of Egypt into the Soviet orbit. He did indeed invite the Ikhwan to return home, as Riedel indicates. Sadat knew the Brothers were bad news, but—much like today's geopolitical big thinkers—he hubristically believed he could control the damage, betting that the Ikhwan would be more a thorn in the side of the jilted Nasserite Communists than a nuisance for the successor regime. Riedel's readers may not appreciate what a naïve wager that was, since he fails to mention that the Brotherhood eventually murdered Sadat in a 1981 coup attempt—in accordance with a fatwa issued by Sheikh Omar Abdel Rahman (later of World Trade Center-bombing fame) after Sadat made peace with the hated "Zionist entity."

Sadat's successor, Mubarak, is undeniably a tyrant who has kept emergency powers in force through the three decades since Sadat's assassination. Any fair assessment, however, must concede that he has had his reasons. Egypt is not just plagued by economic stagnation and inequality; it has been brutalized by jihadist terror. It would be fair enough—though by no means completely convincing—for Riedel and others to argue that Mubarak's reign has been overkill. It makes no sense, though, to ignore both the reason emergency powers were instituted in the first place and the myriad excuses jihadists have given Mubarak to maintain them.

On that score, the Brotherhood seems comparatively moderate, if only because the most horrific atrocities have been committed by two even worse terrorist organizations—Abdel Rahman's Gamaat al Islamia and Ayman al-Zawahiri's Islamic Jihad, both precursors to al-Qaeda (in which Zawahiri is bin Laden's deputy). Of course, Zawahiri—like bin Laden and such al-Qaeda chieftains as 9/11 architect Khalid Sheikh Mohammed—came of age as a Muslim Brother, and Abdel Rahman notoriously had a close working relationship with the Ikhwan. But even if we close our eyes to the Ikhwan's contributions to terrorist violence in Egypt since its attempted forcible overthrow of the regime in 1981, we must not overlook the sophisticated game the Ikhwan plays when it comes to terrorism.

Occasionally, the Brotherhood condemns terrorist attacks, but not because it regards terrorist violence as wrong per se. Instead, attacks are criticized either as situationally condemnable (al-Qaeda's 1998 embassy bombings, though directed at American interests, killed many Muslims and were not supported by an authoritative fatwa), or as counterproductive (the 9/11 attacks provoked a backlash that resulted in the invasion and occupation of Muslim countries, the killing of many Muslims, and severe setbacks to the cause of spreading Islam). Yet, on other occasions, particularly in the Arab press, the Ikhwan embraces violence—fueling Hamas and endorsing the murder of Americans in Iraq.

Our see-no-Islamic-evil foreign-policy establishment blathers on about the Brotherhood's purported renunciation of violence.

In addition, the Brotherhood even continues to lionize Osama bin Laden. In 2008, for example, "Supreme Guide" Muhammad Mahdi Akef lauded al-Qaeda's emir, saying that bin Laden is not a terrorist at all but a "mujahid," a term of honor for a jihad warrior. The Supreme Guide had "no doubt" about bin Laden's "sincerity in resisting the occupation," a point on which he proclaimed bin Laden "close to Allah on high." Yes, Akef said, the Brotherhood opposed the killing of "civilians"—and note that, in Brotherhood ideology, one who assists "occupiers" or is deemed to oppose Islam is not a civilian. But Akef affirmed the Brotherhood's support for al-Qaeda's "activities against the occupiers."

By this point, the Ikhwan's terror cheerleading should surprise no one—no more than we should be surprised when the Brotherhood's sharia compass, Sheikh Yusuf Qaradawi, approves suicide bombings or unleashes rioting over mere cartoons; no more than when the Ikhwan's Hamas faction reaffirms its foundational pledge to destroy Israel. Still, just in case it is not obvious enough that the "Brotherhood renounces violence" canard is just that, a canard, consider Akef's explicit call for jihad in Egypt just two years ago, saying that the time "requires the raising of the young people on the basis of the principles of jihad so as to create mujahideen [there's that word again] who love to die as much as others love to live, and who can perform their duty towards their God, themselves, and their homeland." That leitmotif—*We love death more than you love life*—has been a staple of every jihadist from bin Laden through Maj. Nidal Hasan, the Fort Hood killer.

To this day, the Brotherhood's motto remains, "Allah is our objective, the Prophet is our leader, the Koran is our law, Jihad is our way, and dying in the way of Allah is our highest hope. Allahu akbar!" Still, our see-no-Islamic-evil foreign-policy establishment blathers on about the Brotherhood's purported renunciation of violence—and never you mind that, with or without violence, its commitment is, as Qaradawi puts it, to "conquer America" and "conquer Europe." It is necessary to whitewash the Ikhwan's brutal legacy and its tyrannical designs in order to fit it into the experts' paradigm: history for simpletons. This substitute for thinking holds that, as Secretary of State Condoleezza Rice famously told an Egyptian audience in 2005, America has too often opted for stability rather than freedom. As a result, the story goes, our nation has chosen to support dictators when we should have been supporting . . . never mind that.

The Obama administration has courted Egyptian Islamists from the start.

But we have to mind that. History is rarely a Manichean contest between good and evil. It's not a choice between the pro-Western shah and Iranian freedom, but between the shah and Khomeini's ruthless Islamist revolution. It's not a choice between the pro-Western Musharraf and Pakistani freedom, but between Musharraf and a tense alliance of kleptocratic socialists and Islamists. Back in the 1940s, it was not a choice between the British-backed monarchy and Egyptian freedom, but between the monarchy and a conglomeration of Nasserite pan-Arab socialists, Soviet Communists, and Brotherhood Islamists. And today, the choice is not between the pro-

American Mubarak and Egyptian freedom; it is a question of whether to offer tepid support to a pro-American dictator or encourage swift transition to a different kind of tyranny—one certain to be a lot worse for us, for the West at large, and for our Israeli ally: the Muslim Brotherhood tempered only, if at all, by Mohamed ElBaradei, an anti-American leftist who willfully abetted Iran's nuclear ambitions while running the International Atomic Energy Agency.

History is not a quest for freedom. This is particularly true in the Islamic ummah, where the concept of freedom is not reasoned self-determination, as in the West, but nearly the opposite: perfect submission to Allah's representative on earth, the Islamic state. Coupled with a Western myopia that elevates democratic forms over the culture of liberty, the failure to heed this truth has, in just the past few years, put Hamas in charge of Gaza, positioned Hezbollah to topple the Lebanese government, and presented Islamists with Kosovo—an enduring sign that, where Islam is concerned, the West can be counted on to back away even from the fundamental principle that a sovereign nation's territorial integrity is inviolable.

The Obama administration has courted Egyptian Islamists from the start. It invited the Muslim Brotherhood to the president's 2009 Cairo speech, even though the organization is officially banned in Egypt. It has rolled out the red carpet to the Brotherhood's Islamist infrastructure in the U.S.—CAIR, the Muslim American Society, the Islamic Society of North America, the Ground Zero mosque activists—even though many of them have a documented history of Hamas support. To be sure, the current administration has not been singular in this regard. The courting of Ikhwan-allied Islamists has been a bipartisan project since the early 1990s, and elements of the intelligence community and the State Department have long agitated for a license to cultivate the Brotherhood overtly. They think what Anwar Sadat thought: Hey, we can work with these guys.

There is a very good chance we are about to reap what they've sown. We ought to be very afraid.

Forget the Brotherhood. It's Egypt's Generals Who Should Worry Us

Mehdi Hasan

Mehdi Hasan is a contributing writer for the New Statesman, *a British magazine that focuses on current affairs, world politics, and the arts.*

Should we be worried by the Muslim Brotherhood's victory in the Egyptian presidential election? Earlier this year, I interviewed Wael Ghonim, the young Google executive and anti-Mubarak activist who became the face of Egypt's inspiring revolution back in January and February of 2011.

Was he concerned by the Muslim Brotherhood's victory in Egypt's parliamentary elections in December? "No," he said. "The western media, and even some sections of the Arab media, are taking a very pessimistic view. But what is going on here is very healthy. The Muslim Brotherhood was the strongest party and got almost 50 per cent of the seats." He argued: "We should give democracy a chance and respect the choices of the Egyptian people."

Six months on, Ghonim remains hopeful. "1st elected civilian in modern history of Egypt as President," he tweeted, after the Muslim Brotherhood's Mohammed Morsi's cliffhanger victory over the Mubarak loyalist and ex-premier Ahmed Shafiq in the presidential run-off on 24 June. "Critical milestone. Revolution isn't an event, it's a process so it continues!"

There is a stark contrast between the undimmed optimism of Ghonim—the young, secular, liberal Egyptian activist—and the pessimism of western politicians and pundits, petrified by the rise of the dastardly Muslim Brotherhood. The latter, the world's oldest and most influential Islamist movement, is seen by many as a threat to women's rights, non-Muslims and, of course, western interests in the Middle East.

Bigger Picture

We need to take a collective step back and look again at the big picture. The Arab world's most populous nation has, for the first time, elected its own head of state in a multi-candidate, free and fair election. The repulsive Hosni Mubarak and his corrupt sons are gone; their 30-year reign of terror is over. Lest we forget, in 2006, Morsi was in prison and Mubarak was in the presidential palace; today, just six years later, Mubarak is in prison and Morsi is in the palace. This is a remarkable and historic moment for Egypt, and for the wider Arab world.

The changes we want to see in the Middle East won't happen overnight. Revolutions . . . take time.

That said, Morsi is far from perfect. He wasn't even the Muslim Brotherhood's first choice as presidential candidate (the party's deputy chairman, Khairat al-Shater, was barred from standing). Morsi is a 9/11 conspiracy theorist ("Something must have happened from the inside," he declared in May 2010) who has said that the state should enforce sharia law and has called for women and Christians to be banned from running for president.

But we shouldn't write him off—yet. On winning the election, he promptly quit the Brotherhood, pledged to be the "president of all Egyptians" and promised to appoint a cabinet of "technocrats", not card-carrying Islamists.

Here in the west, however, our obsession with Muslim Brothers such as Morsi distracts attention from two points.

First, the changes we want to see in the Middle East won't happen overnight. Revolutions, as Ghonim pointed out, take time. Yet there seems to be a willful amnesia on the part of some pessimistic pundits in the west.

At a recent Oxford Union debate on the future of the Arab spring, a retired US general, Keith Dayton, decried the ongoing discrimination against women, homosexuals and religious minorities in countries such as Egypt and Libya. I couldn't help but point out to the good general that it took his own country, "the land of the free", 89 years, between independence in 1776 and the passage of the Thirteenth Amendment in 1865, to abolish slavery. Here in the UK, there was a 96-year gap between the first Reform Act of 1832, which extended the franchise to property owners, and the sixth Reform Act of 1928, which gave women the vote on the same terms as men.

Shamefully, the United States has spent the past three decades propping up Egypt's generals.

Second, the most powerful man in Egypt is not President-Elect Morsi but Field Marshal Hussein Tantawi, the chairman of the Supreme Council of the Armed Forces (SCAF), which, in effect, has ruled Egypt since Mubarak left office on 11 February 2011.

It is the military that dominates modern Egyptian politics. All four presidents since a group of officers overthrew the monarchy in 1952 have come from the military. The country's armed forces—the world's tenth-biggest—are believed to control between 30 and 40 per cent of the Egyptian economy. And in June SCAF dissolved the elected parliament and claimed legislative power for itself. Egypt, in the words of one commentator, is a military with a state rather than a state with a military.

Making Waives

Shamefully, the United States has spent the past three decades propping up Egypt's generals. Since the 1979 Egypt-Israel peace treaty, the US has lavished $35bn in aid on the Egyptian military, making it the largest recipient of US military and economic aid after Israel.

But things have changed since the fall of Mubarak, right? Wrong. "Once imperilled, US aid to Egypt is restored", read the headline in the *New York Times* on 23 March. In December 2011, President Obama signed a law that required the Egyptian government to support the transition to civilian government and protect freedoms of speech and assembly before any US military aid could be approved. But, said the *NYT*, Secretary of State Hillary Clinton "used her authority under the new law to waive a requirement that she certify Egypt's protection of human rights", thereby allowing "the Egyptian military to continue to arm and equip its forces". So much for Obama's vow, in May 2011, "to promote reform across the region, and to support transitions to democracy".

The biggest obstacles to greater freedom and democracy in Egypt are the generals, not the Brothers. Yet they, too, like their former boss Mubarak, as well as their paymasters in the US, are on the wrong side of history. The "reform genie", as an unnamed western diplomat told the *Financial Times* on 20 June, is out of the bottle. The Egyptian people, whether secularist or Islamist, Muslim or Christian, won't tolerate another three decades of Mubarak-style rule. As Ghonim told his half-million followers on Twitter in June: "The only thing that will make us go back to living in fear, oppression and silence is a time machine—they haven't invented that yet."

Egyptians Rethink Religion and Politics as They Vote

Lucy Chumbley

Lucy Chumbley is a journalist based in Washington, DC.

As Egyptians vote to elect their next president, what are they looking for? While Western media focus on the role of religious parties and worry about unrest, a University of Maryland poll released on May 21 at the Brookings Institution shows Egyptians are looking toward a more nuanced model for religion and politics—and that there are reasons to be optimistic about Egypt's political transition.

Introducing the findings of the 2012 Public Opinion Survey in Egypt, conducted May 4–10 ahead of the Egyptian presidential debate, principal investigator Shibley Telhami, Senior Fellow at Brookings and the Anwar Sadat Professor for Peace and Development at the University of Maryland, identified presidential candidates Abdel Moneim Aboul Fotouh, formerly affiliated with the Muslim Brotherhood, and Amr Moussa, Egypt's former Minister of Foreign Affairs and Secretary-General of the Arab League, as frontrunners.

The top criteria Egyptians identified as being important in their next president were personal trust in the candidates and their position on the economy, with the role of religion in politics and party affiliation at the bottom of the list.

Though religion was not a deciding factor in the choice of candidates, Telhami said, 66 percent of those questioned favored using shariah as the basis of Egyptian law. But of that number, just 17 percent said it should be interpreted literally, with 83 percent advocating adapting it to contemporary times.

"Shariah is very important psychologically for most Muslims, but the way they interpret it is flexible", Telhami said. Although religion remains important for Egyptians, the role it will take when it comes to the legal system is yet unknown. The fact that Egyptians do not see Islamic principles as monolithic or immutable is a point that those observing the country would do well to remember as the country transitions.

The Egyptian people are looking at their political system holistically, evidenced by the fact that they are differentiating between the president and Parliament.

When asked about what role religion should play in the political system, 54 percent of respondents identified Turkey as the model which most closely matched their aspirations from the choices offered: Iran, Turkey, Tunisia, Malaysia and Morocco. Turkey also emerged as a leading influence in other areas: Outside Egypt, 63 percent of respondents identified Turkish Prime Minister Recep Tayyip Erdogan as the leader they most admired in an open question, while in a question that did not exclude Egyptian leaders, Erdogan came third after former Egyptian presidents Anwar Sadat and Gamal Abdel Nasser.

In a world where there could be just one superpower (Egypt excluded), 41 percent of those polled said they would like to see Turkey in that place.

"The Turkish model clearly is the one that resonates most so far with Egyptians," Telhami said.

Beyond the role of religion and politics, the poll indicates that the Egyptian people are looking at their political system holistically, evidenced by the fact that they are differentiating between the president and Parliament, he added.

While Egyptians listed personal trust, the economy, and track record and experience as being most important in determining how they will vote in the presidential elections, the key factors determining their choices in the parliamentary elections were different. Here, the political party was seen as most important, followed by record, experience and the economy.

Noting that the poll's results are indicative of trends rather than election results due to the lack of benchmarking data, Telhami pointed out that these findings for the most part track the conventional wisdom in Egypt, though the political situation continues to be "fluid."

Most Egyptians he consulted "were not surprised by the results," he said: "It matched the general perception."

Conducted using a nationally representative stratified sample of 773 people from cities and rural areas, the poll was carried out via professional face-to-face interviews.

"Most political parties are really behind peaceful mobilization," Telhami said, noting that Egypt—a country of 80 million—has come a long way in the last year and a half. "That's pretty optimistic stuff, I think."

Good Government Does Not Have to Be Secular

Elizabeth Shakman Hurd

Elizabeth Shakman Hurd is an assistant professor of political science at Northwestern University in Evanston, Illinois. She speaks and writes frequently on Middle East politics and religion issues and is the author of The Politics of Secularism in International Relations *(2007).*

It is striking the extent to which the word "secular"—and related terms such as secular democracy and secular leaders—are relatively synonymous with all that is good, right and universal in many Western accounts of developments in Egypt.

The indiscriminate association of the secular with good governance and the natural domain of rational self-interest and universalist ethics contrasts with the idea of Islam as irrational and decidedly not secular.

But as history plays out so dramatically in the Middle East, it is time to replace such simplistic views of Muslim-majority societies with a much more complicated story about religion and politics in Egypt.

A History of Repressions

The Muslim Brotherhood, founded in 1928 and still officially outlawed in Egypt, is anxiously depicted in these accounts as "Islamist" and represented as a potential danger that might result from the emergence of democracy in Egypt. Political positions expressed through reference to Islamic tradition, history, or politics are assimilated into the category of "bad" politics and assumed to threaten normal, rational, and democratic politics. Political Islam is seen as a throwback to pre-modern forms of Muslim political order.

Washington remained silent as the Mubarak regime arrested hundreds of Brothers and transferred dozens to military courts.

Thus, aligning Western interests with a secular dictator has been seen as preferable to encouraging democratic measures that would accommodate the interests of so-called unreliable and dangerous Islamists.

The United States has stood forcefully and famously behind this state-instituted and highly securitized secular-religious oppositional binary as a means of defending its interests in the region. These are defined primarily as ensuring Israeli security, pursuing the war on terror, and guaranteeing access to oil.

After Egypt's 2005 parliamentary elections, in which the Muslim Brotherhood gained one-fifth of the seats in parliament, U.S. pressure on the [Hosni] Mubarak regime decreased and then ceased entirely after Hamas' victory in 2006. Washington remained silent as the Mubarak regime arrested hundreds of Brothers and transferred dozens to military courts.

No Reason to Fear Islamic Government

But today the Egyptian people and a powerful anti-Mubarak coalition are overturning this entire structure of domination, upheld by Mubarak and aided and abetted by the Americans and the Europeans for decades. The future is up for grabs.

Misguided Western constructs of Islamist politics have empowered Mubarak and other autocrats throughout the region. Such thinking fails to address the realities of contemporary politics in states in which these movements have gained a strong and legitimate political foothold. These cannot be washed away by wishful thinking in Washington, London, or Jerusalem.

Such a hostile attitude toward the Muslim Brotherhood also is unfounded. According to Nathan Brown, "a lot of their program is just standard reform stuff—independence of the judiciary, the end of corruption, protecting the environment. Especially when they got more political over the last 10 years or so, what they really began to push was a very general reform language that takes Islamic coloration in some areas. But an awful lot of it is consistent with other reform programs coming from reformists all over the political spectrum."

It remains to be seen whether Western decision-makers and pundits will display the political courage and intellectual creativity needed to move beyond the false choice between secular dictators and "crazy Islamists" and support real democracy in the Middle East, for a change. The opposite of democratic is not Islamic. It is military dictatorship.

CHAPTER 4

How Should the United States Balance Religion and Politics in the Future?

Chapter Preface

Although the First Amendment's guarantee of freedom of religion and separation of church and state have been part of American law for more than two centuries, there is still debate in America about how religion should be balanced with secular government interests. Historically, the US Supreme Court has closely scrutinized any government action that infringes on First Amendment rights, including freedom of religion. However, the Supreme Court decisions on religion in the 1980s shifted towards allowing the government to restrict religious freedom as long as the government action treated all religions the same way. This trend upset many religious organizations and civil rights groups, and led to the passage in 1993 of the Religious Freedom Restoration Act (RFRA)—legislation that required governments to have a compelling state interest before limiting freedom of religion. This law basically reinstated the earlier Supreme Court approach of strict scrutiny to government actions affecting religion. However, the Supreme Court later ruled the RFRA unconstitutional as it applied to state and local governments, a decision that continues to be controversial today.

The so-called strict scrutiny test required by the RFRA was clearly set forth by the Supreme Court in two cases—*Sherbert v. Verner* (1963) and *Wisconsin v. Yoder* (1972). These cases mandated that courts must find a compelling government interest in order to justify a substantial burden on freedom of religion. Under this test, to be compelling, a government interest must involve relatively important concerns that rise above mere bureaucratic or efficiency goals. Examples of compelling government interests might include national security, protecting citizens' lives, or preserving other constitutional protections. Another part of the strict scrutiny test is that the government must use the least restrictive means to achieve its goal. If the government action that infringes on religious freedom is overbroad, it can still be overturned even if it is a compelling interest.

Later cases weakened the strict scrutiny test in cases involving issues of religion. The main example is the case of *Employment Division v. Smith* (1990), where the Supreme Court ruled that the government could deny unemployment benefits to a person fired for using peyote, an illegal hallucinogenic drug, even though the peyote was used as part of a native American religious ceremony. This and other cases established the principle that the government could restrict religious freedom by passing or enforcing laws of general applicability that apply to all religions without discrimination.

The RFRA, signed into law on November 16, 1993, was a reaction to this looser interpretation of freedom of religion and sought to reinstate the *Sherbert* strict scrutiny test. The question of whether the RFRA was constitutional soon became the subject of a number of lawsuits, and eventually the case of *Boerne v. Flores* reached the Supreme Court. In *Boerne*, the Court was presented with the question of whether a local government's refusal to allow the Roman Catholic Archdiocese of San Antonio to expand a church in Boerne, Texas, violated the RFRA. The Archdiocese argued that the city's denial of a permit to tear down part of the church and expand it to accommodate a growing congregation (because it was located in a historic district) was a substantial burden on freedom of religion without a compelling state interest. The Supreme Court, in a June 1997 decision, ruled that the RFRA was unconstitutional as applied to state and local governments because it exceeded Congress' constitutional enforcement powers. The RFRA, the Court explained, was an attempt by Congress to expand freedom of religion by proscribing government conduct that the constitution does not prohibit. Justice John Paul Stevens clarified the issue when he pointed out that if the church in question happened to be owned by an atheist, there would be no question that the city could deny the permit; thus, the Catholic Church should not get a special exemption from a generally applicable, neutral civil law.

Since the *Boerne* decision, however, a number of states—including Alabama, Arizona, Connecticut, Florida, Idaho, Illinois, New Mexico, Rhode Island, South Carolina, and Texas—have enacted laws patterned after the RFRA. In other states, such as California, Illinois, and Virginia, these types of bills have failed. Critics have challenged these laws as violations of the separation of church and state because they favor religious groups over non-religious groups. Another concern has been that prisoners could use RFRA-type state laws to file frivolous lawsuits claiming that their religious rights are being violated by the restrictions of their imprisonment. At the federal level, the US Congress has also considered but rejected laws that would have replaced the RFRA. The Religious Liberty Protection Act of 2000 (RLPA), for example, passed in the House of Representatives but died in the Senate.

Most notably, although *Boerne* clearly held the RFRA unconstitutional for states and local governments, the law still applies to actions by the federal government. The Supreme Court recently applied the RFRA compelling interest test, for example, in *Gonzales v. O Centro Espirita Beneficente Uniao do Vegetal* (2006), a case that involved the government's seizure of a sacramental tea that contained an illegal drug from a church in New Mexico. The Court found that the government did not have a compelling interest in seizing illegal substances from the church.

Whether the federal RFRA or similar state statutes will herald the birth of expanded protections for freedom of religion in the United States remains to be seen, but it is clear that many religious groups will continue to push for this result. In addition to the RFRA approach, religious advocates are proposing federal- and state-level constitutional amendments to clarify that infringements of religious practices by governments require a compelling state interest. The authors of viewpoints in this chapter discuss these amendments and other issues relevant to how the United States should balance religion and politics in the future.

President Barack Obama Should Support a Constitutional Amendment to Secure Religious Freedom

Rodney K. Smith

Rodney K. Smith is a First Amendment scholar and a professor of law at the Thomas Jefferson School of Law in San Diego, California.

Religious freedom in America is under attack from the right and the left. James Madison, the father of our Constitution, referred to the right of conscience as "the most sacred of all property"—our greatest possession.

That right is increasingly insecure. Under his expansive health care initiative President [Barack] Obama mandated that all institutions provide insurance coverage for contraceptives, including the morning-after pill, even though this mandate violated the religious conscience of Roman Catholics.

The Obama administration narrowly averted a major political crisis when it later agreed to "balance" the government mandate by accommodating the free-exercise rights of Catholics. But now critics say the adjustment doesn't fully exempt the church from funding coverage for birth control, calling it a "shell game." And leaders in the Catholic church have said the compromise amounts to a "hill of beans" and have vowed legal action.

Religious Freedom Under Attack

What is clear is that Mr. Obama had the power—and still does—to disregard the right of conscience, if political winds

Rodney K. Smith, "Does Obama Really Care About Religious Freedom in America?" *Christian Science Monitor*, February 17, 2012. Copyright © 2012 by Rodney K. Smith. All rights reserved. Reproduced by permission.

blew in another direction. Does the president really support the freedom of conscience or is his gesture a politically motivated charade?

Perhaps, but the trend away from religious freedom has been under attack long before the Obama decision.

In 1990, Justice [Antonin] Scalia, a conservative member of the Supreme Court, authored a decision in *Employment Division v. Smith*, a case considering whether the state of Oregon could deny unemployment benefits to two Native American men for their use of peyote (a cactus with psychoactive properties when ingested), whose use and possession is illegal in the state, in the Native American Church.

It isn't hard to predict that government will eventually extend its regulatory tentacles into private faith-based education, health care, and even social services.

With his ruling, Mr. Scalia rejected past Court precedent that provided stronger protection for the right of religious conscience—precedent that had served our nation well. Largely ignoring the track record under the old rule, his opinion stated that to exempt the men from penalties for their religious use of peyote would "make the professed doctrines of religious belief superior to the law of the land, and in effect to permit every citizen to become a law unto himself."

Scalia essentially enunciated a new rule that permits the federal government to violate religious conscience so long as it does so with a general law that is not directly intended to discriminate against religious exercise. In that single act, the Court reduced religious conscience from a right to a mere privilege.

The response to Scalia's opinion was dramatic. Congress, overwhelmingly and with strong support from President [Bill] Clinton, passed the Religious Freedom Restoration Act of 1994, restoring a robust right of conscience. Unfortunately, in

City of Boerne v. Flores, decided in 1997, the Court held that Congress had exceeded it powers, effectively leaving Obama free to disregard religious conscience in his health care initiative.

With the growth of government, religious conscience will likely continue to fall victim to these so-called general laws. It isn't hard to predict that government will eventually extend its regulatory tentacles into private faith-based education, health care, and even social services.

An Old Conflict

This conflict over religious freedom and the reach of government is not new. George Mason and James Madison disagreed over the scope of the right of religious conscience when Virginia was adopting a declaration of rights.

Mason and Madison both acknowledged that religion is a duty owed our Creator. Mason, however, believed that while religious conscience "should enjoy the fullest toleration," government was free to regulate conscience if it "disturb[ed] the peace, the happiness, or safety of society."

[James] Madison understood what [US Supreme Court Justice Antonin] Scalia and [Barack] Obama evidently do not, that conscience is our most significant possession.

Alarmed that Mason had transformed the most sacred of rights into a mere privilege granted by tolerant lawmakers, Madison responded that free exercise could only be limited when the exercise of that right deprived another of an "equal liberty" and when that exercise of conscience "manifestly endangered" the "existence of the state."

For Mason, like Obama and Scalia, religious exercise was a privilege at the mercy of government. Madison, however, saw it as an inalienable right largely beyond the reach of government. Madison's view became the basis for our First Amendment.

Madison understood what Scalia and Obama evidently do not, that conscience is our most significant possession.

Dr. Martin Luther King, Jr., had an experience during the early stages of the civil rights movement that demonstrated the importance of the right of conscience.

One night, Dr. King received a vicious call threatening his family. As he worried about his family, he realized "religion had to become real . . . [he] had to know God for [himself]." He prayed, "Lord, I'm down here trying to do what's right. . . . I think the cause we represent is right. But Lord . . . I'm losing my courage. And I can't let the people see me like this because if they see me weak . . . they will begin to get weak."

King heard an inner voice saying, "Martin Luther, stand up for righteousness. Stand up for justice. Stand up for truth. And lo I will be with you, even until the end of the world." He was "called" to lead a movement that transformed America.

Recognizing the importance of conscience King taught that, "If you haven't found something worth dying for, you aren't fit to be living."

Madison would see Dr. King's religious conscience as a right, not a mere gift from an occasionally tolerant government. It seems that Obama would have us believe that he would recognize it as a right as well, but his actions indicate he may not.

The Need for a Constitutional Amendment

If Obama, Scalia, and others continue their overreach and disregard for this fundamental right of conscience, religious freedom in America will remain insecure. If Obama genuinely supports religious liberty, he can step forward and offer his support for an amendment adopting the language of the Religious Freedom Restoration Act of 1994.

That amendment would restore religious liberty by requiring that the government prove that its regulation of religious exercise is necessary to a compelling state interest. The amendment would also require the government to prove that the regulation is the least restrictive manner in which the government's compelling interest can be achieved.

That amendment would recognize that religious liberty is not a mere privilege. It would restore our most sacred possession—the *right* of religious conscience.

Religious Rights vs. the Public's Right

Oliver Thomas

Oliver Thomas is an author and a member of the board of contributors for USA Today, *a daily national newspaper.*

Religion is a tricky business. It can bring out the best in a person. Think Mahatma Gandhi, Albert Schweitzer or Mother Teresa. But it can also bring out the worst. Think 9/11, the Inquisition or the Salem witch trials. What I'm saying is that religion can short-circuit your ability to think. You sometimes can't see things as they really are because irrational beliefs get in the way. I'll give you a couple of examples.

In New York, ultra-Orthodox Jews are criticizing the Brooklyn district attorney for prosecuting Jewish child sex-abuse cases, according to *The New York Times*. The newspaper reports that a 16-year-old ultra-Orthodox Jewish boy was being molested in a Jewish ritual bathhouse in Brooklyn. After his father reported the crime to police, the father said he was shunned, cursed and kicked out of his apartment by other ultra-Orthodox Jews for trying to protect his son.

In California, inmate Billy Paul Birdwell argued that his religion, Asatru-Odinism, required him to have open space and a fire pit. Prison officials gave him the open space and even built a fence around it. But when officials later replaced that space with a non-denominational outdoor area, Birdwell complained that his religious needs weren't met. Starting to get the picture? To people living within a particular religious tradition, the beliefs always seem reasonable. But there are limits to how far we as a nation can go in protecting the rights of citizens to exercise their faith.

A Step Too Far

Now, North Dakota is getting into the act by pushing for a state constitutional amendment to allow for even more religious freedom. If approved by voters on June 12, the change could result in even more bizarre outcomes over religion.

For decades, the U.S. employed a test for deciding these cases that balanced the religious liberty rights of the individual against the public's right to maintain a civil society. The test went like this. If the government placed a "substantial burden" on a person's religiously motivated behavior, the government must show that the burden was (1) in furtherance of a "compelling" interest, such as health and safety, and (2) was the least burdensome means of accomplishing that interest. The test worked well for years. Religious claimants won some and lost some. Then the Supreme Court changed the rules.

In a case involving the use of peyote by Native Americans, the high court held that it was no longer necessary for government to justify restrictions on religious exercise unless the religion was being singled out for discriminatory treatment.

Of course, legislative bodies generally don't single out particular religions for special burdens. They pass laws that say no one can drink wine in a particular county, and suddenly Catholics have a problem celebrating the Mass. Or they say everyone has to wear a hard hat, and Sikhs—who must wear a turban instead—can no longer get a construction job. Nearly all burdens on religious exercise are caused by laws of general application.

States Take Priority

So you can guess what happened. Religious groups began having problems. Government, to a large measure, stopped accommodating religious exercise. Congress corrected the problem through the "Religious Freedom Restoration Act"—which returned things to the way they were before the peyote ruling. But the Supreme Court would not allow Congress to correct the states. That had to be done by the states themselves. Some 16 legislatures have done precisely that. In other places, the state Supreme Court has stepped in to provide similar protections by interpreting their own constitutions in ways that protect religious exercise.

Either way, America is the better for it. Orthodox Jewish boys can wear their yarmulkes to school, Muslim girls can wear their head scarves, Jewish prisoners can get a kosher meal and evangelical Christians can home-school their children without fear of reprisal from the state.

But some religious Americans want more. Unsatisfied with the First Amendment balancing test, they now want to tilt the playing field. Several states are considering these more radical remedial measures.

North Dakota's proposed constitutional amendment, for example, would eliminate the requirement that a government-imposed burden be "substantial." Any burden would trigger strict scrutiny. The amendment states that even "indirect" burdens, such as withholding benefits, assessing penalties or excluding people from programs would be prohibited. So not only may you home-school your child, you might even be able to force taxpayers to pay for your child to attend a parochial school.

If this is making you nervous, it should. It carries a faint odor of theocracy. Religious freedom may be the crown jewel of our 236-year-old experiment in liberty, but few of us would like to return to Puritan New England. Perhaps it is time for lovers of liberty, including religionists of all stripes, to say "enough."

Religious Institutions Operating Public Accommodations Must Obey Secular Laws

Armando Lloréns-Sar

Armando Lloréns-Sar is a feature writer for the Daily Kos, *a political blog that publishes news and commentary from a progressive viewpoint.*

In 2006, then-Sen. Barack Obama gave a speech on religion in the public square. Obama said:

> Conservative leaders have been all too happy to exploit this gap, consistently reminding evangelical Christians that Democrats disrespect their values and dislike their Church, while suggesting to the rest of the country that religious Americans care only about issues like abortion and gay marriage; school prayer and intelligent design.

> Democrats, for the most part, have taken the bait. At best, we may try to avoid the conversation about religious values altogether, fearful of offending anyone and claiming that—regardless of our personal beliefs—constitutional principles tie our hands.

> At worst, there are some liberals who dismiss religion in the public square as inherently irrational or intolerant, insisting on a caricature of religious Americans that paints them as fanatical, or thinking that the very word "Christian" describes one's political opponents, not people of faith.

I consider it one of Obama's worst speeches ever. On the substance, it is nonsense—accepting of Republican nostrums on "what Democrats think," and then proposing ridiculous ideas for "religion in the public square." As a question of politics, it was a failure as its intent was to inoculate Obama from attack on "lack of faith" grounds from the "Religious Right." Kenyan socialist Muslim anyone? But if that speech was the end of it, well, politics is what it is. But it has not ended there.

[Journalist] E.J. Dionne, joining the most radical elements of the "Religious" Right, has led the "progressive" Catholic attack on the principle of separation of church and state. Dionne points to Obama's 2006 speech as the beacon to follow on this issue, rejecting in essence the famous formulations of JFK's 1960 speech on the issue.

The Encroachment of Religion into Government

The encroachment of religion on our secular government proceeds at an alarming pace.

Last Thursday, the United States Senate narrowly rejected, by a 51-48 vote, passage of the Blunt Amendment, also known as the "Respect for Rights of Conscience Act." The amendment would:

> [Amend] the Patient Protection and Affordable Care Act (PPACA) to permit a health plan to decline coverage of specific items and services that are contrary to the religious beliefs of the sponsor, issuer, or other entity offering the plan or the purchaser or beneficiary (in the case of individual coverage) without penalty. [...] Declares that nothing in PPACA shall be construed to authorize a health plan to require a provider to provide, participate in, or refer for a specific item or service contrary to the provider's religious beliefs or moral convictions. Prohibits a health plan from being considered to have failed to provide timely or other

access to items or services or to fulfill any other requirement under PPACA because it has respected the rights of conscience of such a provider.

Prohibits an American Health Benefit Exchange (a state health insurance exchange) or other official or entity acting in a governmental capacity in the course of implementing PPACA from discriminating against a health plan, plan sponsor, health care provider, or other person because of an unwillingness to provide coverage of, participate in, or refer for, specific items or services.

The separation of church and state . . . insure[s] free exercise of religion and protect[s] the secular government from the encroachment of religion.

To its credit, the Obama administration opposed the Blunt Amendment:

A proposal being considered in the Senate this week would allow employers that have no religious affiliation to exclude coverage of any health service, no matter how important, in the health plan they offer to their workers. This proposal isn't limited to contraception nor is it limited to any preventive service. Any employer could restrict access to any service they say they object to. This is dangerous and wrong.

The Obama administration believes that decisions about medical care should be made by a woman and her doctor, not a woman and her boss. We encourage the Senate to reject this cynical attempt to roll back decades of progress in women's health.

No word on what E.J. Dionne thinks. However, the Obama administration could be accused of betraying the 2006 words of Sen. Obama by "try[ing] to avoid the conversation about religious values altogether, fearful of offending anyone and claiming that—regardless of our personal beliefs—constitutional principles tie our hands." After all, if you provide "accommodations" to religiously affiliated institutions regarding their conduct in the secular world, why not to religious persons as well?

The failure was in not championing the separation of church and state as a principle designed to insure free exercise of religion and protect the secular government from the encroachment of religion. This approach protects religion and the state. It is a principle worth fighting for and being proud of the fight. Instead, the Obama administration is now down the path of a convoluted morass of deciding when, and when not to, accommodate religion in our secular government. The line should be easy to find.

In a recent case, much touted by supporters of the Blunt Amendment, the Supreme Court explained where the line should be drawn. The case is *Hosanna-Tabor Evangelical Lutheran Church and School v. Equal Employment Opportunity Commission et al.* Writing for a unanimous Court, Chief Justice [John] Roberts stated:

> Until today, we have not had occasion to consider whether this freedom of a religious organization to select its ministers is implicated by a suit alleging discrimination in employment. The Courts of Appeals, in contrast, have had extensive experience with this issue. Since the passage of Title VII of the Civil Rights Act of 1964, 42 U. S. C. §2000e et seq., and other employment discrimination laws, the Courts of Appeals have uniformly recognized the existence of a "ministerial exception," grounded in the First Amendment, that precludes application of such legislation to claims concerning the employment relationship between a religious institution and its ministers. We agree that there is such a ministerial exception. The members of a religious group put their faith in the hands of their ministers.
>
> Requiring a church to accept or retain an unwanted minister, or punishing a church for failing to do so, intrudes

upon more than a mere employment decision. Such action interferes with the internal governance of the church, depriving the church of control over the selection of those who will personify its beliefs. By imposing an unwanted minister, the state infringes the Free Exercise Clause, which protects a religious group's right to shape its own faith and mission through its appointments.

When a religion decides that it will own public accommodations, such as hospitals, it must abide by our secular laws and regulations.

Religion in the Secular World

When it comes to the religious institution itself and its function as a ministry, the state has no role and must have no role. Thus a religion can choose to not ordinate women or persons of color as ministers. It can apply discriminatory rules in all aspects of its religious institutions, insisting that women be segregated from men, both in the place of worship or on transportation vehicles operated for purposes of the religious institution. (To be sure, the Court is not particularly consistent in application of this principle.)

However, when the religious institution chooses to engage in the secular world, regulated by our secular government, this protection from government regulation and law ends. Thus, when the Hasidim of Brooklyn choose to use public transportation, they are not permitted to enforce their discriminatory views that women must ride in the back of the bus.

When a religion decides that it will own public accommodations, such as hospitals, it must abide by our secular laws and regulations. This is the crucible of the issue today. Consider this *New York Times* editorial:

A wave of mergers between Roman Catholic and secular hospitals is threatening to deprive women in many areas of the country of ready access to important reproductive services. Catholic hospitals that merge or form partnerships with secular hospitals often try to impose religious restrictions against abortions, contraception and sterilization on the whole system.

Here is the line, easy for all to see. The imposition of religion on a secular public accommodation should not be countenanced. In this case, it involves the Catholic Church imposing religious limitations on health care for women at a public hospital. In the case of the Blunt Amendment, the principle is extended to religious persons, not just institutions.

The Proper Role of Religion in Politics

This does not mean that religions and religious persons must be out of the public arena. To the contrary, religions and religious people should be in the arena, like all of us, fighting for our respective views.

I would expect, and defend the right of, religions and religious persons to work to have their views enshrined in our laws. Thus, for those religions who oppose birth control and women's right to choose, I expect them to fight for the overturn of *Griswold v. Connecticut* and *Roe v. Wade*. For those religions who believe in discrimination based on gender, race or sexual orientation, I expect them to be in the public arena fighting for secular laws that encompass their views on these subjects. And for the positive, for those religions and their adherents who oppose the death penalty, aggressive war, and unbridled capitalism, I expect them to be in the public arena fighting for their views.

My expectations are met every day. No religion and no religious person has been excluded nor do they act as if they have been excluded from the public arena. What some demand however is that even when they lose the argument in the public arena, that they get an exception from following our secular laws. That is unacceptable.

It is a principle that no progressive should even contemplate, much less accept. And yet, too many do. Many Democrats and progressives have, to coin a phrase, "taken the bait." We now see more clearly where that path is leading us. It is an unacceptable path.

The United States Should Promote the Christian Ideals of Religious Freedom and Democracy Around the World

Charles J. Chaput

Charles J. Chaput is the archbishop of Denver, Colorado. From 2003 to 2006, he served as a commissioner with the United States Commission on International Religious Freedom (USCIRF), an independent, bipartisan federal body that monitors violations of religious freedom abroad and makes recommendations to the president, the secretary of state, and the Congress.

In his World Day of Peace message earlier this year [2011], Pope Benedict XVI voiced his concern over the worldwide prevalence of "persecution, discrimination, terrible acts of violence and religious intolerance." In reality, we now face a global crisis in religious liberty. As a Catholic bishop, I have a natural concern that Christian minorities in Africa and Asia bear the brunt of today's religious discrimination and violence. Benedict noted this same fact in his own remarks.

But Christians are not the only victims. Data from the Pew Forum on Religion and Public Life are sobering. Nearly 70 percent of the world's people now live in nations—regrettably, many of them Muslim-majority countries, as well as China and North Korea—where religious freedom is gravely restricted.

Principles that Americans find self-evident—the dignity of the human person, the sanctity of conscience, the separation of political and sacred authority, the distinction between secular and religious law, the idea of a civil society pre-existing and distinct from the state—are not widely shared elsewhere. In fact, as Leszek Kolakowski once said, what seemed self-evident to the American Founders "would appear either patently false or meaningless and superstitious to most of the great men that keep shaping our political imagination." We need to ask ourselves why this is the case.

We cannot understand the framework of American institutions . . . if we don't acknowledge that they grow out of a predominantly Christian worldview.

We also need to ask ourselves why we Americans seem to be so complacent about our own freedoms. In fact, nothing guarantees that America's experiment in religious freedom, as we traditionally know it, will survive here in the United States, let alone serve as a model for other countries in the future. The Constitution is a great achievement in ordered liberty. But it's just another elegant scrap of paper unless people keep it alive with their convictions and lived witness.

Yet in government, media, academia, in the business community and in the wider culture, many of our leaders no longer seem to regard religious faith as a healthy or a positive social factor. We can sense this in the current administration's ambivalence toward the widespread violations of religious liberty across the globe. We can see it in the inadequacy or disinterest of many of our news media in reporting on religious freedom issues. And we can see it especially in the indifference of many ordinary American citizens.

In that light. I have four points that I'd like to share with you today. They're more in the nature of personal thoughts than conclusive arguments. But they emerge from my years as a Commissioner with the U.S. Commission on International Religious Freedom (USCIRF). and I believe they're true and need to be said. The first three deal with the American experience. The last one deals with whether and how the American experience can apply internationally.

A Christian Worldview

Here's my first point: *The American model of religious liberty is rooted in the thought-world and idea-architecture of the Christian humanist tradition.* We cannot understand the framework of American institutions—or the values that these institutions are meant to promote and defend—if we don't acknowledge that they grow out of a predominantly Christian worldview.

Obviously our laws and public institutions also reflect Jewish scripture, Roman republican thought and practice, and the Enlightenment's rationalist traditions. But as Crane Brinton once observed with some irony, even "the Enlightenment [itself] is a child of Christianity—which may explain for our Freudian times why the Enlightenment was so hostile to Christianity."

The American system of checks and balances, which emphasizes personal responsibility and limited government, reflects fundamental biblical truths.

Whatever it becomes in the future, America was *born* Protestant. And foreign observers often seem to understand that better than we do. As many of you know, Dietrich Bonhoeffer, the German Lutheran scholar and pastor murdered by the Third Reich, taught for a time in New York City in the 1930s. He came away struck by the differences between the American and French revolutionary traditions, and the Christian character of American ideals.

"American democracy," Bonhoeffer said, "is not founded upon the emancipated man but, quite on the contrary, upon the kingdom of God and the limitation of all earthly powers by the sovereignty of God."

As Bonhoeffer saw it, the American system of checks and balances, which emphasizes personal responsibility and limited government, reflects fundamental biblical truths about original sin, the appetite for power and human weakness.

Jacques Maritain, the French Catholic scholar who helped draft the U.N.'s charter on human rights, said much the same. He called our Declaration of Independence "an outstanding lay Christian document tinged with the philosophy of the day."

He also said: "The [American] Founding Fathers were neither metaphysicians nor theologians, but their philosophy of life, and their political philosophy, their notion of natural law and human rights, were permeated by concepts worked out by Christian reason and backed up by an unshakeable religious feeling."

That's my point. At the heart of the American model of public life is a Christian vision of man, government and God.

Now, I want to be clear about what I'm saying here—and also what I'm *not* saying.

I'm *not* saying that America is a "Christian nation." Nearly 80 percent of our people self-describe as Christians. And many millions of them actively practice their faith. But we never have been and never will be a Christian confessional state.

I'm *also* not saying that our Protestant heritage is uniformly good. Some of the results clearly *are* good: America's culture of personal opportunity; respect for the individual; a tradition of religious liberty and freedom of speech; and a reverence for the law. Other effects of Reformation theology have been less happy: radical individualism; revivalist politics; a Calvinist hunger for material success as proof of salvation; an ugly nativist and anti-Catholic streak; a tendency toward intellectual shallowness and disinterest in matters of creed; and a nearly religious, and sometimes dangerous, sense of national destiny and redemptive mission.

None of these sins however—and yes, some of our nation's sins have led to very bitter suffering both here and abroad—takes away from the genius of the American model. This model has given us a free, open and non-sectarian society marked by an astonishing variety of cultural and religious expressions. But our system's success does not result from the procedural mechanisms our Founders put in place. Our system works *precisely* because of the moral assumptions that undergird it. And those moral assumptions have a *religious* grounding.

The American Bill of Rights is not a piece of 18th-century rationalist theory: it is far more the product of Christian history.

Human Rights Guaranteed by God

That brings me to my second point: *At the heart of the American model of religious liberty is a Christian vision of the sanctity and destiny of the human person.*

The great Jesuit scholar, Father John Courtney Murray, stressed that: "The American Bill of Rights is not a piece of 18th-century rationalist theory: it is far more the product of Christian history. Behind it one can see, not the philosophy of the Enlightenment, but the older philosophy that had been the matrix of the common law. The 'man' whose rights are guaranteed in the face of law and government is, whether he knows it or not, the Christian man, who had learned to know his own dignity in the school of Christian faith."

I believe that's true. It's a crucial insight. And it's confirmed by other scholarship, including Harold Berman's outstanding work in the history of Western law, and his study of religious liberty and America's founding. My point here is that the institutions and laws in what we call the "Western world" presume a Christian anthropology; a Christian definition of the meaning of life. In the American model, the human person is not a product of nature or evolution. He is not a creature of the state or the economy. Nor, for that matter, is he the slave of an impersonal heaven. Man is first and fundamentally a *religious* being with intrinsic worth, a free will and inalienable rights. He is created *in the image of* God, *by* God and *for* God. Because we are born for God, we belong to God. And any claims that Caesar may make on us, while important, are secondary.

In the vision of America's Founders, God endows each of us with spiritual freedom and inherent rights so that we can fulfill our duties toward him and each other. Our rights come from God, not from the state. Government is justified only insofar as it secures those natural rights, promotes them and defends them.

And this is not just the curious view of some religious shaman. Nearly all the men who drew up our founding documents held this same belief. Note what James Madison said in his "Memorial and Remonstrance against Religious Assessments" in 1785:

"[Man's duty of honoring God] is precedent both in order of time and degree of obligation to the claims of civil society. Before any man can be considered as a member of civil society, he must be considered as a subject of the Governor of the universe."

The American logic of a society based on God's sovereignty ... has also proven itself remarkably capable of self-criticism, repentance, reform and renewal.

That is why *religious* freedom is humanity's first and most important freedom. Our first governor is God, our Creator, the Governor of the universe. We are created for a religious purpose. We have a religious destiny. Our right to pursue this destiny *precedes* the state. Any attempt to suppress our right to worship, preach, teach, practice, organize and peacefully engage society because of our belief in God is an attack not only on the cornerstone of human dignity, but also on the identity of the American experiment.

I want to add one more thing here: The men who bequeathed us the American system, including the many Christians among them, had a legion of blind spots. Some of those flaws were brutally ugly—slavery, exploitation of the Native peoples, greed, and ethnic and religious bigotry, including a crude anti-Catholicism that remains the most vivid religious prejudice this country has ever indulged.

But the American logic of a society based on God's sovereignty and the sanctity of the human person has also proven itself remarkably capable of self-criticism, repentance, reform and renewal.

Religion Essential to U.S. Democracy

This brings me to my third point: *In the American model, religion is more than a private affair between the individual believer and God. Religion is essential to the virtues needed for a free people. Religious groups are expected to make vital contributions to the nation's social fabric.*

The American experience of personal freedom and civil peace is inconceivable without a religious grounding, and a specifically Christian inspiration.

For all their differences, America's Founders agreed that a free people cannot remain free and self-governing without religious faith and the virtues that it fosters. John Adams' famous words to the Massachusetts militia in 1789 were typical: "Our constitution was made only for a moral and religious people. It is wholly inadequate to the government of any other."

When the Founders talked about religion, they meant something much more demanding and vigorous than the vague "spirituality" in vogue today. Harold Berman showed that the Founders understood religion in a frankly Christian-informed sense. Religion meant "both belief in God and belief in an after-life of reward for virtue, and punishment for sin." In other words, religion *mattered*—personally and socially. It was more than a private preference. It made people *live differently*. People's faith was assumed to have broad implications, including the political kind.

From the beginning, believers—alone and in communities—have shaped American history simply by trying to live their faith in the world. As Nathaniel Hawthorne saw so well, too many of us do it badly, with ignorance and hypocrisy. But enough believers in every generation have done it well enough, long enough, to keep the animating spirit of our country's experiment in ordered liberty alive.

Or to put it another way, the American experience of personal freedom and civil peace is inconceivable without a religious grounding, and a specifically Christian inspiration. What we believe about God shapes what we believe about man. And what we believe about man shapes what we believe about the purpose and proper structure of human society.

The values enshrined in the American model touch the human heart universally.

The differences among Christian, atheist, Hindu, Jewish and Muslim thought are not "insurmountable." *But they are also not "incidental."* Faith, sincerely believed or sincerely refused, has consequences. As a result, theology and anthropology have serious, long term, social and political implications. And papering those differences over with a veneer of secular pieties does *not* ensure civil peace. It ensures conflict—because religious faith touches on the most fundamental elements of human identity and destiny, and its expression demands a public space.

Applying Christian Values to Other Countries

This brings me to my fourth and final point: *I believe that the American model does work and that its principles can and should be adapted by other countries.* But with this caveat. The Christian roots of our ideals have implications. It's impossible to talk honestly about the American model of religious freedom without acknowledging that it is, to a significant degree, the product of Christian-influenced thought. Dropping this model on non-Christian cultures—as our country learned from bitter experience in Iraq—becomes a very dangerous exercise. One of the gravest mistakes of American policy in Iraq was to overestimate the appeal of Washington-style secularity, and to underestimate the power of religious faith in shaping culture and politics.

Nonetheless, I do believe that the values enshrined in the American model touch the human heart universally. We see that in the democracy movements now sweeping the Middle East and North Africa. The desires for freedom and human dignity live in all human beings. These yearnings are not culturally conditioned, or the result of imposed American or Western ideals. They're inherent to all of us.

The modern world's system of international law is founded on this assumption of universal values shared by people of all cultures, ethnicities and religions. The Spanish Dominican priest, Francisco de Vitoria, in the 16th century envisioned something like the United Nations. An international rule of law is possible, he said, because there is a "natural law" inscribed in the heart of every person, a set of values that are universal, objective, and do not change. John Courtney Murray argued in the same way. The natural law tradition presumes that men and women are religious by nature. It presumes that we are born with an innate desire for transcendence and truth.

These assumptions are at the core of the 1948 Universal Declaration of Human Rights. Many of the people who worked on that Declaration, like Jacques Maritain, believed that this charter of international liberty reflected the American experience.

Article 18 of the Declaration famously says that "Everyone has the right to freedom of thought, conscience and religion; this right includes freedom to change his religion or belief; and freedom, either alone or in community with others and in public or private, to manifest his religion or belief in teaching, practice, worship and observance."

A healthy distinction between the sacred and the secular, between religious law and civil law, is foundational to free societies.

In a sense, then, the American model has already been applied. What we see today is a repudiation of that model by atheist regimes and secular ideologies, and also unfortunately by militant versions of some non-Christian religions. The global situation is made worse by the inaction of our own national leadership in promoting to the world one of America's greatest qualities: religious freedom.

This is regrettable because we urgently need an honest discussion on the relationship between Islam and the assumptions of the modern democratic state. In diplomacy and in interreligious dialogue we need to encourage an Islamic public theology that is both faithful to Muslim traditions and also open to liberal norms. Shari'a law [Islamic law] is not absolution. Christians living under shari'a uniformly experience it as offensive, discriminatory and a grave violation of their human dignity.

A healthy distinction between the sacred and the secular, between religious law and civil law, is foundational to free societies. Christians, and especially Catholics, have learned the hard way that the marriage of Church and state rarely works. For one thing, religion usually ends up the loser, an ornament or house chaplain for Caesar. For another, *all theocracies are utopian*—and every utopia ends up persecuting or murdering the dissenters who can't or won't pay allegiance to its claims of universal bliss. . . .

The Pilgrim's Progress . . . [John Bunyan's book about the Puritans, early settlers in North America] is the second most widely read book in the Western world, next only to the Bible. But the same Puritan spirit that created such beauty and genius in Bunyan also led to Oliver Cromwell, the Salem witch trials and the theocratic repression of other Protestants and, of course, Catholics.

Americans have learned from their own past. The genius of the American founding documents is the balance they achieved in creating a civic life that is non-sectarian and open to all: but also dependent for its survival on the mutual respect of secular and sacred authority. The system works. We should take pride in it as one of the historic contributions this country has made to the moral development of people worldwide. We need to insist that religious freedom—a person's right to freely worship, preach, teach and practice what he or she believes, including the right to freely change or end one's religious beliefs under the protection of the law—is a foundation stone of human dignity. No one, whether acting in the name of God or in the name of some political agenda or ideology, has the authority to interfere with that basic human right.

This is the promise of the American model. The Founders of this country, most of them Christian, sought no privileges for their kind. They would not force others to believe what they believed. Heretics would not be punished. They knew that the freedom to believe must include the freedom to change one's beliefs or to stop believing altogether. Our Founders did not lack conviction. Just the opposite. They had enormous confidence in the power of their own reason—but also in the sovereignty of God and God's care for the destiny of every soul.

America was born, in James Madison's words, to be "an asylum to the persecuted and oppressed of every nation and religion." Right now in America, we're not acting like we revere that legacy, or want to share it, or even really understand it.

And I think we may awake one day to see that as a tragedy for ourselves, and too many others to count.

Organizations to Contact

The editors have compiled the following list of organizations concerned with the issues debated in this book. The descriptions are derived from materials provided by the organizations. All have publications or information available for interested readers. The list was compiled on the date of publication of the present volume; the information provided here may change. Be aware that many organizations take several weeks or longer to respond to inquiries, so allow as much time as possible.

Berkley Center for Religion, Peace, & World Affairs
3307 M St., Suite 200, Washington, DC   20007
(202) 687-5119
e-mail: berkleycenter@georgetown.edu
website: http://berkleycenter.georgetown.edu/rfp

The Berkley Center for Religion, Peace, & World Affairs is a project located at Georgetown University in Washington, DC. It is dedicated to the interdisciplinary study of religion, ethics, and public life through research, teaching, and service. The center explores issues such as the global challenges of democracy and human rights; economic and social development; international diplomacy; and interreligious understanding. The center affirms that a deep examination of faith and values is needed and that the open engagement of religious and cultural traditions with one another can promote peace. The center's website provides book recommendations and is a source for other publications, including papers and articles such as "The Role of Civil Society in Peacebuilding, Conflict Resolution, and Democratization," "Law, Religion, and Liberty of Conscience," and "Water and Faith: Rights, Pragmatic Demands, and an Ethical Lens."

Council on Foreign Relations (CFR)
1777 F St. NW, Washington, DC   20006
(202) 509-8400 • fax: (202) 509-8490
website: www.cfr.org

The Council on Foreign Relations (CFR) is an independent, nonpartisan membership organization, think tank, and publisher. It is composed of more than seventy full-time and adjunct fellows who cover the major regions of the world and important foreign policy issues shaping the current international agenda. CFR publishes in various formats, including videos and transcripts of talks with world leaders and policymakers, the bimonthly magazine *Foreign Affairs*, and numerous articles and op-eds. Examples include "Religion and Politics in America" and "Islam and Politics."

The Heritage Foundation
214 Massachusetts Ave. NE, Washington, DC   20002-4999
(202) 546-4400
website: www.heritage.org

The Heritage Foundation is a conservative think tank that researches, formulates, and promotes conservative policies based on the principles of free enterprise, limited government, individual freedom, and a strong national defense. The foundation's targeted audiences include members of Congress, key congressional staff members, policymakers in the executive branch, national news media, and the academic and policy communities. The Heritage Foundation website is a source of many articles, including "Obama v. Religious Liberty: How Legal Challenges to the HHS Contraceptive Mandate Will Vindicate Every American's Right to Freedom of Religion," "Defending Religious Liberty for All," and "Let Religious Freedom Ring: Stop the Assault on Our First Freedom."

Institute on Religion & Democracy (IRD)
1023 Fifteenth St. NW, Suite 601
Washington, DC   20005-2601
(202) 682-4131 • fax: (202) 682-4136
e-mail: info@theird.org
website: www.theird.org

The Institute on Religion & Democracy (IRD) is an ecumenical alliance of American Christians working to reform their churches' social programs in accord with biblical Christian teachings and to contribute to the renewal of a democratic society at home and abroad. IRD is committed to biblical and traditional teachings, to upholding democratic freedoms in the United States, and extending those freedoms to persecuted and oppressed people around the world. IRD publishes *Faith & Freedom*, a bimonthly magazine covering church news, religious liberty, and social witness topics, and *UMAction Briefing*, a quarterly newsletter for United Methodists working for church renewal. Both of these are available on the IRD website, along with a series of papers on public policy issues. Examples include "What Is the Most Important Environmental Task Facing American Christians Today?" and "Is Marriage Worth Defending?"

Pew Forum on Religion & Public Life

1615 L St. NW, Suite 700, Washington, DC   20036
(202) 419-4550
website: http://projects.pewforum.org

The Pew Forum on Religion & Public Life is a project of the Pew Research Center, a nonpartisan fact tank. The project tries to promote a deeper understanding of issues at the intersection of religion and public affairs by conducting surveys, demographic analyses, and other social science research on important aspects of religion and public life in the United States and around the world. The project also provides a neutral venue for discussions of timely issues through roundtables and briefings. The project's website contains links to numerous publications relevant to religion and politics, including: "Little Voter Discomfort with Romney's Mormon Religion," "Catholics Share Bishops' Concerns about Religious Liberty," and "Public Views of the Divide Between Religion and Politics."

Politics of Religious Freedom

e-mail: pennyismay@berkeley.edu
website: http://iiss.berkeley.edu

Politics of Religious Freedom is a three-year project (2011–2014) designed to examine how religious freedom is being transformed through legal and political processes in the United States, the Middle East, South Asia, and the European Union. Funded by the Henry R. Luce Initiative on Religion and International Affairs, the project is based at the University of California, Berkeley, and at Northwestern University in Evanston, Illinois, and it is also affiliated with Indiana University in Bloomington and University of Maryland Law in Baltimore. The project works with academics, key human rights and civil society organizations, and jurists and policymakers. The project's website is a source of various publications on religion and politics. Examples include "Good Muslim, Bad Muslim," "Believing in Religious Freedom," and "Religious Freedom, Minority Rights, and Geopolitics."

Bibliography

Books

David Brody — *The Teavangelicals: The Inside Story of How the Evangelicals and the Tea Party Are Taking Back America.* Grand Rapids, MI: Zondervan, 2012.

Walter Brueggemann — *The Practice of Prophetic Imagination: Preaching an Emancipatory Word.* Minneapolis, MN: Fortress Press, 2012.

E.J. Dionne Jr. — *Our Divided Political Heart: The Battle for the American Idea in an Age of Discontent.* New York: Bloomsbury USA, 2012.

Colonel V. Doner — *Christian Jihad: Neo-Fundamentalists and the Polarization of America.* Littleton, CO: Samizdat Creative, 2012.

Robert Booth Fowler et al. — *Religion and Politics in America: Faith, Culture, and Strategic Choices.* Boulder, CO: Westview Press/Perseus Books Group, 2010.

Jonathan Haidt — *The Righteous Mind: Why Good People Are Divided by Politics and Religion.* New York: Pantheon Books/Random House, 2012.

Charles Kimball — *When Religion Becomes Lethal: The Explosive Mix of Politics and Religion in Judaism, Christianity, and Islam.* San Francisco, CA: Jossey-Bass/Wiley, 2011.

Stéphane Lacroix — *Awakening Islam: The Politics of Religious Dissent in Contemporary Saudi Arabia.* Cambridge, MA: Harvard University Press, 2011.

Frank Lambert — *Religion in American Politics: A Short History.* Princeton, NJ: Princeton University Press, 2008.

Mark Lilla — *The Stillborn God: Religion, Politics, and the Modern West.* New York: Knopf, 2007.

Andrew C. McCarthy — *The Grand Jihad: How Islam and the Left Sabotage America.* New York: Encounter Books, 2012.

Pippa Norris and Ronald Inglehart — *Sacred and Secular: Religion and Politics Worldwide.* Cambridge, UK: Cambridge University Press, 2004.

Matt Taibbi — *The Great Derangement: A Terrifying True Story of War, Politics, and Religion at the Twilight of the American Empire.* New York: Spiegel & Grau, 2008.

Monica Duffy Toft, Daniel Philpott, and Timothy Samuel Shah — *God's Century: Resurgent Religion and Global Politics.* New York: Norton, 2011.

| Kenneth D. Wald and Allison Calhoun-Brown | *Religion and Politics in the United States.* Lanham, MD: Rowman & Littlefield, 2010. |
| Robert Wuthnow | *Red State Religion: Faith and Politics in America's Heartland.* Princeton, NJ: Princeton University Press, 2012. |

Periodicals and Internet Sources

David E. Campbell and Robert D. Putnam	"God and Caesar in America: Why Mixing Religion and Politics Is Bad for Both," *Foreign Affairs*, March/April 2012. www.foreign affairs.com.
Catholic League for Religious and Civil Rights	"Okay to Mix Politics and Religion," June 29, 2012. www.catholic league.org.
CBS News	"Andrew Sullivan: There's So Much Bad Religion Right Now," April 7, 2012. www.cbsnews.com.
Timothy M. Dolan	"ObamaCare and Religious Freedom," *Wall Street Journal*, January 25, 2012.
Richard Allen Greene	"Religious Persecution Is Widespread, Report Warns," CNN, April 29, 2010. http://articles.cnn.com.
Gary Gutting	"The Opinionator: Should Religion Play a Role in Politics?" *New York Times*, July 27, 2011.

Kate Hicks   "Obama vs. Catholics: The War on Religious Freedom," Townhall.com, February 7, 2012. http://townhall.com.

John Hilton   "Will 'Teavangelicals' Turn the Obama/Romney Tide?" Belief and Beyond, July 9, 2012. www.york blog.com/faith.

Elizabeth Shakman Hurd   "The Tragedy of Religious Freedom in Syria," *Chicago Tribune News*, March 29, 2012. http://articles.chicagotribune.com.

Charles C. Johnson   "Understanding Obama: Why Muslims Get Religious Freedom and Catholics Need Not Apply," *Breitbart*, February 15, 2012. www.breitbart.com.

Jaweed Kaleem   "Religion and Politics Don't Mix, Major Religious Groups Tell Presidential Candidates," *Huffington Post*, February 21, 2012. www.huffingtonpost.com.

Meris Lutz   "Majority of Muslims Want Islam in Politics, Poll Says," *Los Angeles Times*, December 6, 2010. http://articles.latimes.com.

Barry Lynn   "On Faith: The Role Religion Should Play in Republican Politics," *Washington Post*, August 19, 2011. www.washingtonpost.com.

Eric Marrapodi   "5 Reasons 'Teavangelicals' Matter,"
                        CNN Belief Blog, June 27, 2012.
                        http://religion.blogs.cnn.com.

Jonathan Merritt   "The Religious Right Turns 33: What
                        Have We Learned?" *The Atlantic*, June
                        8, 2012. www.theatlantic.com.

John J. Myers   "The Opinion Pages: Religious
                        Freedom: An American Bishop's
                        View," *New York Times*, May 25,
                        2012. www.nytimes.com.

Nicole Neroulias   "American Politics More Religious
                        than American Voters," *Huffington
                        Post*, August 22, 2012. www
                        .huffingtonpost.com.

New York Times   "The Politics of Religion," May 27,
                        2012. www.nytimes.com.

Barack Obama   "Politicians Need Not Abandon
                        Religion," *USA Today*, July 9, 2006.
                        www.usatoday.com.

PBS Newshour   "Romney and 'Teavangelicals':
                        Gaining Trust with Conservative
                        Voters," July 10, 2012. www.pbs.org
                        /newshour.

Kirsten Powers   "America's Naivete About Egypt," *The
                        Daily Beast*, February 3, 2011.
                        www.thedailybeast.com.

Reince Priebus   "Obama's Assault on Religious
                        Freedom," *Politico*, February 8, 2012.
                        http://dyn.politico.com.

Winnifred Fallers Sullivan — "We Are All Religious Now. Again," *Social Research*, Vol. 76, No. 4, Winter 2009.

Winnifred Fallers Sullivan, Elizabeth Shakman Hurd, and Peter Danchin — "The Global Securitization of Religion," Social Science Research Council, March 23, 2010. http://blogs.ssrc.org.

Loretta Sword — "Should Religion Play a Role in Politics?" *Pueblo Chieftain*, February 11, 2012. www.chieftain.com.

Scott M. Thomas — "A Globalized God: Religion's Growing Influence in International Politics," *Foreign Affairs*, November/December 2010. www.foreignaffairs.com.

Index

A

Abortion issues
    health care and, 60–61
    opposition to, 21, 22–23
    program funding and, 63
    religion and, 40, 41–42
    support for, 26
Adams, John, 146
Addington, David, 58
Affordable Care Act, 84
Afghanistan, 93
African American Protestants, 47, 49, 51
Ahmadiyah Muslim sect, 91
Aid to the Church in Need charity, 90
Akef, Muhammad Mahdi, 106
Algeria, 97
American Health Benefit Exchange, 135
American Muslims, 55
American Revolution (1775–1783), 17
Anglican Church. *See* Church of England
Anti-Semitism, 54, 103
Arab Spring, 67, 88
Asatru-Odinism, 130
Atheists
    Christianity and, 147
    in communism, 93, 96
    government and, 149
    as religious, 25, 122

B

Bailey, Sarah Pulliam, 60–65
al-Banna, Hassan, 101–103
Bannister, Andy, 89–96
Baptists, 18, 21
Becket Fund for Religious Liberty, 57
Pope Benedict XVI, 140
Berman, Harold, 144, 147
Bhatti, Shahbaz, 94
Bibi, Asia, 94
The Bible, 16, 40, 72
Bill of Rights (US), 18, 144
bin Laden, Osama, 101, 105, 106, 107
Birdwell, Billy Paul, 130
Blaire, Stephen, 80
Blasphemy laws in Pakistan, 94
Bloomberg, Michael, 55
Blunt Amendment. *See* Respect for Rights of Conscience Act
Boerne v. Flores, 122, 123
Boggs, Lilburn, 54–55
Bonhoeffer, Dietrich, 142–143
Boston College, 75
Boston Tea Party (1773), 21
Brinton, Crane, 142
Brody, David, 21, 23
Brookings Institution, 114
Brown, Nathan, 119
Brownfield, Mike, 56–59
Brueggemann, Walter, 29–34
Buddhism, 86, 96
Bunyan, John, 150
Bush, George W., 22–23, 70

At Issue

Do Infectious Diseases Pose a Threat?

Other Books in the At Issue Series:

At Issue

|Do Infectious Diseases
|Pose a Threat?

Roman Espejo

GREENHAVEN PRESS
A part of Gale, Cengage Learning

GALE
CENGAGE Learning·

Detroit • New York • San Francisco • New Haven, Conn • Waterville, Maine • London

Elizabeth Des Chenes, *Director, Content Strategy*
Cynthia Sanner, *Publisher*
Douglas Dentino, *Manager, New Product*

For more information, contact:
Greenhaven Press
27500 Drake Rd.
Farmington Hills, MI 48331-3535
Or you can visit our Internet site at gale.cengage.com

Articles in Greenhaven Press anthologies are often edited for length to meet page requirements. In addition, original titles of these works are changed to clearly present the main thesis and to explicitly indicate the author's opinion. Every effort is made to ensure that Greenhaven Press accurately reflects the original intent of the authors. Every effort has been made to trace the owners of copyrighted material.

© Images.com/Corbis

LIBRARY OF CONGRESS CATALOGING-IN-PUBLICATION DATA

Do infectious diseases pose a threat? / Roman Espejo, book editor.
    pages cm. -- (At issue)
    Includes bibliographical references and index.
    ISBN 978-0-7377-6830-5 (hardcover) -- ISBN 978-0-7377-6831-2 (pbk.)
  1. Communicable diseases. 2. Emerging infectious diseases. 3. Pathogenic micro-organisms. 4. Epidemiology. I. Espejo, Roman, 1977- editor of compilation.
  RA643.D595 2014
  362.1969--dc23
                                        2013009119

Printed in the United States of America
1 2 3 4 5 6 7 17 16 15 14 13

Contents

Introduction

Modern-day medicine and advancements have made significant strides against malaria. Over the past decade, deaths from the infectious disease have dropped 30 percent around the globe. For instance, in Sri Lanka—locked in a fierce civil war for twenty-six years—malaria has been all but eradicated, reduced by 99.9 percent since 1999. Researchers from the nation's Anti-Malaria Campaign and the University of California, San Francisco, highlight the effectiveness of strategies used to reach those who lived in conflict zones, such as the dispatch of mobile clinics to remote populations and, when it was too dangerous to spray homes with insecticide, the delivery of specially treated nets. "There is no silver bullet for malaria elimination," says Gawrie Galappaththy of the Anti-Malaria Campaign. "Instead, it's a daily commitment to finding the cases, treating the patients and preventing transmission," she explains.[1]

Malaria was eliminated from North America in 1951—now just seen in travelers and military servicemembers stationed abroad—and the World Health Organization (WHO) announced that Europe was free of the disease in 1975. It was first controlled with an insecticide called DDT (dichlorodiphenyltrichloroethane) in the 1960s, which has been globally banned in agriculture. Currently, treatment protocols include artemisinin, a plant-based drug that was originally used in China for centuries to treat fever, as well as lumefantrine, an antibiotic that remains in the body for one week. Chloroquine, the predecessor of artemisinin, was the first-line malaria drug until widespread resistance developed against it by the 1990s.

---

1. Quoted in "Malaria Nearly Eliminated in Sri Lanka Despite Decades of Conflict," *UC Health*, August 29, 2012. http://health.universityofcalifornia.edu/2012/08/29/malaria-nearly-eliminated-in-sri-linka-despite-decades-of-conflict.

Despite progress, malaria continues to persist in developing countries. More than 650,000 people die annually from the disease, largely in sub-Saharan Africa. "Few Americans appreciate how devastating malaria is to the third world. AIDS gets more press, but malaria . . . killed huge numbers of Africans and crippled development efforts,"[2] writes author Bryan Burrough in *The New York Times*. Malaria is spread by *Anopheles gambiae*, a species of mosquito that thrives in warm and humid climates, when carrying parasites from the *Plasmodium* family. Its five known species are found in tropical and subtropical areas in the world; the deadliest is *Plasmodium falciparum*, which makes up more than three-fourths of infections in Africa. A mosquito becomes infected by biting an infected person and, in turn, infects other people by biting them. Depending on the species of the parasite, symptoms can appear between nine and forty days and include fever, chills, sweating, headache, fatigue, nausea, and vomiting.

Recently, concerns have been raised surrounding the emergence of drug-resistant malaria. It was first recognized in Cambodia in 2008, but a 2012 study from the medical journal *Lancet* found that artemisinin took increasingly longer times to fight off the parasites in Thai patients treated from 2001 to 2010. "We are going to see patients that don't respond to the treatment anymore,"[3] maintains Francois Nosten, a doctor who oversees the Shoklo Malaria Research Unit, a part of the Faculty of Tropical Medicine at Mahidol University in Thailand. According to Nosten, in some instances artemisinin requires three to four days to clear the parasite from the body—not the expected twenty-four hours. "We have to beat this

2. Bryan Burrough, "Of Management and Mosquito Nets," *New York Times*, August 20, 2011. www.nytimes.com/2011/08/21/business/in-lifeblood-management-lessons-in-foreign-aid.html.
3. Quoted in Ian Williams, "Drug-Resistant Malaria in Thailand Threatens a Deadly Global 'Nightmare,'" worldnews.nbcnews.com, January 2, 2013. http://worldnews.nbcnews.com/_news/2013/01/02/15903518-drug-resistant-malaria-in-thailand-threatens-deadly-global-nightmare?lite.

resistance, win this race, and eliminate the parasite before it's too late. That's our challenge now," he insists.

A vaccine for malaria does not yet exist, but some experts are hopeful that one will be developed in the near future, especially with the specter of drug resistance. In a 2011 clinical trial, a vaccine candidate from GlaxoSmithKline (GSK) provided children up to seventeen months old 55 percent protection against malaria and 47 percent protection against severe malaria. "We would have wished that we could wipe it out, but I think this is going to contribute to the control of malaria rather than wiping it out,"[4] asserts Tsiri Agbenyega, a principal investigator in the trials. Nonetheless, in trials the following year, the same drug did not match these results in babies under twelve weeks old, offering 31 percent protection against malaria and 37 percent against severe malaria. "The slightly lower than expected efficacy will . . . affect the cost-benefit analysis that health providers and funders will have to undertake before deciding whether the vaccine represents the best use of limited financial resources,"[5] maintains Eleanor Riley, an immunology professor at the London School of Hygiene and Tropical Medicine. With support for the vaccine candidate's potential, more trials are slated for 2014. "If a million babies were vaccinated, we would prevent 260,000 cases of malaria a year,"[6] reasons Moncef Slaoui, chairman of research and development at GSK.

From the impacts on impoverished populations in developing countries to the pharmaceutical quandary of drug resistance, malaria represents some of the complex and enormous

4. Quoted in Kate Kelland and Ben Hirschler, "World's First Malaria Vaccine Works in Major Trial," Reuters, October 18, 2011. www.reuters.com/article/2011/10/18/us-malaria-vaccine-gsk-idUSTRE79H58T20111018.

5. Quoted in Kate Kelland and Ben Hirschler, "Setback for First Malaria Vaccine in African Trial," Reuters, November 9, 2012. www.reuters.com/article/2012/11/09/us-malaria-vaccine-gsk-idUSBRE8A80I120121109.

6. Quoted in Donald G. McNeil Jr., "Malaria Vaccine Candidate Gives Disappointing Results," New York Times, November 9, 2012. www.nytimes.com/2012/11/10/health/malaria-vaccine-candidate-produces-disappointing-results-in-clinical-trial.html.

challenges of infectious diseases. In *At Issue: Do Infectious Diseases Pose a Threat?* numerous experts, researchers, and commentators offer their analyses, insights, and doubts on the most feared and devastating pathogens to exist—and those that may possibly emerge.

1

Fighting the Rise of Emerging Infectious Diseases

Corrie Brown and Thijs Kuiken

Corrie Brown is the Josiah Meigs Distinguished Teaching Professor at the University of Georgia's College of Veterinary Medicine. Thijs Kuiken is a professor of comparative pathology at Erasmus Medical Center in The Netherlands.

Emerging infectious diseases (EIDs)—known or closely related agents that occur in new areas or species—with high transmission and mortality rates are on the rise. Animal sources are attributed to 75 percent of all EIDs, such as the avian influenza virus (H5N1), severe acute respiratory syndrome (SARS), and mad cow disease, which are more prevalent due to globalization. Emerging diseases not only threaten animal welfare, public health, and the environment but can also result is massive economic costs, decreased food supplies, and losses to a variety of industries. To prevent an EID from becoming epidemic or pandemic, global health monitoring for humans, livestock, and wildlife must be improved for early detection of outbreaks.

Emerging infectious diseases (EIDs) are on the rise, occurring at an unprecedented rate in animal and human populations, and posing a major threat to the biological safety of our 21st century world. Mother Nature's potential threat may be, in the end, much greater than any destruction that could result from another world war, a nuclear bomb blast, or some heinous act of terrorism. In a worst-case scenario, the emergence of a new infectious disease with high transmissibility and mortality has the potential to devastate the human population before sufficient resources can be rallied effectively. We may have dodged a bullet with H1N1—the so-called swine flu—but have we learned our lesson as to what could have been?

The term "emerging disease" usually describes a known disease or closely related agent appearing in a new geographic area or occurring in a new species. It also could be a previously unknown disease agent detected for the first time.

Because 75% of emerging human diseases worldwide over the past two decades have originated from animal sources, there has been considerable consternation in the public health and veterinary communities. There is a critical need for a surveillance system that thoroughly integrates data on humans with that of wild and domestic animals, as veterinary pathologists often play a key role is the early detection of these EIDs.

"Zoonosis" is the term used to define an animal pathogen that moves into a human host. The highly pathogenic avian influenza virus (H5N1), or bird flu, is just one example of a zoonotic threat to human health and well-being. Others include severe acute respiratory syndrome (SARS), bovine spongiform encephalopathy (BSE) or "mad cow" disease, and the Ebola virus.

Animal welfare, human health, and the environment all suffer as a result of . . . emerging diseases, but economic losses can be even more staggering.

Given the ideal combination of circumstances, all have the potential to become epidemic or pandemic. "Epidemic" describes any widespread outbreak of an infectious disease, while the term "pandemic" typically is reserved for a global outbreak that affects a large proportion of the world's population.

The principal reasons that zoonotic diseases are so much more prevalent today are the increasing numbers of humans and the expanding globalization of trade. International commerce has tripled over the past 20 years, resulting in unprecedented levels of traffic in people, animals, and animal products. That, combined with unrelenting population growth, has created a synergy for microorganisms to move freely and quickly from their commonly inhabited domains into unexpected niches, often with lethal results.

Animal welfare, human health, and the environment all suffer as a result of these emerging diseases, but economic losses can be even more staggering. Owners and producers of animals and animal products experience direct losses from animal treatment costs, deaths, and the resulting decreased production, as well as from restrictions prohibiting the export or importation of infected animals or their by-products. Indirectly, animal diseases affect everyone. Decreased food supplies generally mean higher prices. In addition, there usually are costs related to food safety, the environment, and the prevention and treatment of human disease, plus losses to tourism and other industries.

One of the biggest catalysts for the emergence—and reemergence—of zoonotic diseases is delayed response and reporting.

Avian influenza, for instance, remains a concern. H5N1 quietly began establishing itself in the poultry populations of Asia in the early 1990s. The initial disease was so mild it escaped detection. By 1997, however, the virus had mutated to a form so lethal it could kill chickens within 48 hours. Following a brief outbreak that year, it all but disappeared, only to reemerge in 2003 in a highly pathogenic form. The virus is transmitted primarily through direct or indirect exposure to respiratory secretions or feces of infected birds.

Even if avian influenza is controlled in poultry—as has been done in the U.S.—there still are wild birds to worry about. There was high mortality of free-living birds reported at a breeding site at Qinghai Lake, western China. In Western Europe, there also has been repeated mortality of mute swans—as well as other wild bird species, mainly ducks, geese, and raptors—associated with H5N1 virus infection. This has led to a number of reported deaths among carnivore species, including tigers, leopards, palm civets, and domestic cats. All most likely contracted the virus by feeding on carcasses of infected domestic or wild birds.

Considering that thousands of people must have had contact with infected poultry, the risk of human infection with H5N1 virus in its current form appears to be quite low. The fact that the primary lesion of the infection in humans is located deep in the lungs, instead of the upper respiratory tract, may help to explain this, as well as why human-to-human transmission is so rare.

In theory, however, the H5N1 virus could become transmissible among humans through mutation or reassortment with a human influenza virus. Reassortment could occur in humans, pigs, or another species where both viruses can replicate. Mutation could occur in humans, cats, or other mammalian species. Yet, the likelihood of this is difficult to predict.

One of the biggest catalysts for the emergence—and re-emergence—of zoonotic diseases is delayed response and reporting. Most developing countries neither have the laboratory facilities nor the trained personnel to diagnose the diseases in a timely fashion. Furthermore, once a disease is detected, some nations may be reluctant to report it due to conflicts of interest and the potential negative impact on local economies.

Another huge factor facilitating the spread of animal diseases is lack of sufficient infrastructure to address the outbreak. In many countries, national budgets are so restrictive that surveillance and eradication are problematic. In some instances, when a link to public health can be made, funds oftentimes are liberated more quickly than they may be if it is considered solely an agricultural problem.

Infectious diseases remain a leading cause of death around the world.

A better integrated health monitoring system for humans, livestock, and wildlife is needed. The current surveillance system for animals mainly is the responsibility of government departments of agriculture, which typically do not include wildlife and can vary greatly among countries. Global public health management largely is in the hands of the World Health Organization, Food and Agriculture Organization of the United Nations, and World Organization for Animal Health. The close relationship between animal and human health is pulling these organizations together like never before.

One suggestion includes the creation of an international expert working group to design and implement a global animal surveillance system for zoonotic pathogens that would be integrated closely with public health surveillance. It could be formed in conjunction with organizations such as WHO, FAO, and others. The group's mission would be to provide early warning of pathogen emergence in time to control such pathogens before they can affect human health, food supply, economies, or biodiversity. This group could be charged with identifying the current gaps in surveillance and determining the most cost-effective ways to fill them.

It is paramount that emerging infectious disease outbreaks be reported earlier than in the past—before they become endemic—if we are to have a chance of eliminating them at their source. Once a pathogen becomes endemic, such as the avian flu virus did in large parts of Asia, it becomes very difficult to eradicate by human means.

Infectious diseases remain a leading cause of death around the world. Moreover, it is tough to know where the next pathogen will come from, or when. The challenge remains to expect the unexpected.

$$2$$

Infectious Diseases Threaten National Security

Christopher R. Albon

Christopher R. Albon is project director at FrontlineSMS, a developer of free open source texting software used by humanitarian and political organizations. Albon also writes for the Atlantic, Foreign Policy, and other publications.

Infectious diseases and the military are historically intertwined, and emerging infectious diseases and rising drug resistance in the twenty-first century endanger armed forces and global security. Developing countries are the most vulnerable due to poverty, civil conflict, and weak institutions. For example, rampant HIV/AIDS has devastated African militaries—reducing recruitment pools, experienced personnel, and peacekeeping capacity—as well as creating greater financial burdens. As for national security, infectious diseases threaten regions where Western nations have great stakes in maintaining stability to secure strategic or economic interests. It is recommended that programs help the militaries of developing countries to strengthen their health capacities and assist their foreign allies in responding to outbreaks.

Militaries and infectious diseases have always been intertwined. History records hundreds of armies crippled by disease. In his account of the Peloponnesian War, [Greek historian] Thucydides describes the devastation of a wartime

Christopher R. Albon, "Infectious Diseases and Us National Security," *Current Intelligence*, July 28, 2010. Copyright © 2010 Current Intelligence. All rights reserved. Reproduced by permission.

plague on the Athenian people and leadership. German General Erich Von Ludendorff blamed the 1918 Spanish flu pandemic for failure of his spring offensive and ultimately contributing to the Allied victory. However, after World War II the strategic implications of infectious disease on national security were overlooked. Instead security and foreign policy communities primarily focused on the nuclear tension between the United States and the Soviet Union. . . .

After the Cold War, attempts were made to expand the concept of security into new areas including economic, societal, and health security. The concept of human security has made particular headway. Human security was first posited in the 1994 United Nations Human Development Report and argues security must be redefined in terms of the individual rather than the state. The report lists a number of threats to individuals from famine to environmental destruction. However, while human security's expanded definition has been useful, it is unnecessary in the present discussion. Infectious diseases are also threats in state-centric notions of national security. Diseases can weaken the capacity of militaries in developing states where Western nations have significant enough national interest to respond to internal, external, and regional threats. Securing these states would place additional burdens on resources, but the global risk from new and reemerging infectious diseases continues to rise in the 21st century, with significant implications for global and regional security.

The Growing Importance of Infectious Diseases

The middle of the 20th century saw rapid progress in fighting various diseases. Experts believed new technology had stemmed the spread of many infectious diseases in the developed world and lent hope of high levels of health worldwide by the end of the millennium. However, recently new infectious diseases have emerged and once-controllable diseases have mutated and developed drug resistance.

Globalised trade, a growing and more mobile population, and widespread urbanisation resulted in emerging and re-emerging infectious diseases spreading rapidly at the turn of the century. This "third wave" of infectious diseases—including HIV, cholera, and tuberculosis—have become a significant threat. The 2000 US National Intelligence Estimate classified infectious disease for the first time as a threat to national security, warning, "new and reemerging infectious diseases will pose a rising global health threat and will complicate US and global security." Infectious diseases in the future will thrive in an ever more interconnected, mobile, and crowded world.

The impact of infectious disease has struck hardest in the developing world, where poverty, conflict, and weak institutions leave states vulnerable. As a result, infectious diseases pose the greatest threat to developing states and their militaries. How might infectious diseases weaken the militaries of developing states? Where are they most vulnerable? A strong case study through which to examine these questions is the tragic and ongoing problem of HIV/AIDS in African militaries.

The precise figure is debated but some armed forces are rumored to have HIV prevalence rates over 50%.

Devastating Impact

Few doubt the devastating effect of HIV/AIDS on African militaries. In 2007, around 22 million Africans were infected by the HIV-2 strain, representing two-thirds of worldwide infections. In seven Southern African states, HIV prevalence exceeds 15%.

Militaries personnel are at particular risk of HIV infection, with the majority of recruits between 18 and 24 years old, sexually active, and experiencing long deployments away from traditional social networks amid a military culture that promotes aggression, machismo, and risk taking.

The precise figure is debated but some armed forces are rumored to have HIV prevalence rates over 50%. The South African National Defense Force (SANDF) admits between 10% and 12% of military personnel are HIV-positive, a range many consider conservative. In 2004, China rejected one-third of Zimbabwean officers for advanced training due to their HIV status. HIV prevalence rates in African militaries are unknown or—in some cases—classified as state secrets. However, it is reasonable to assume HIV rates are at least comparable to the state's civilian population and thus high enough to weaken African militaries in numerous ways:

Military personnel with AIDS are less able to complete physically demanding tasks, are more susceptible to adverse conditions during deployments, and have lower morale.

Smaller Recruitment Pool—Recruits who are HIV-positive are seen as less suitable for military service. In response to high HIV prevalence in the general population some African militaries conduct pre-employment testing. However, testing can cause prospective recruits to self-select out of military service, shrinking the recruitment pool and reducing the overall quality of the armed forces.

Loss of Experienced Personnel—The effects of HIV/AIDS are felt all along the chain of command. Half of the Malawian general staff, for example, has been rumored to be HIV positive. South Africa is facing rising HIV prevalence in young blacks while 'fast tracking' young black officers into mid-level positions. Experienced officers take decades to train and develop, making them one of the military's most valuable resources. The loss of experienced personnel to HIV/AIDS erodes African militaries of their organisational capacity and institutional knowledge.

Reduction in Effectiveness—High infection rates weaken the ability of African militaries to operate effectively. Military personnel with AIDS are less able to complete physically demanding tasks, are more susceptible to adverse conditions during deployments, and have lower morale. Furthermore, individuals unable to perform their duties must be transferred to less demanding roles, reducing the capacity of the military to deploy homogenous units.

Greater Financial Burden—African armed forces are primarily reliant on their human resources. However, the mounting financial costs of personnel with HIV/AIDS drains the financial resources of African militaries. Militaries with high HIV prevalence have less financial resources available for their core functions. Professor Lindy Heinecken of South Africa's Stellenbosch University has called this the "biggest challenge" for the SANDF.

Reduced Peacekeeping Capacity—HIV/AIDS weakens the ability of African armed forces to participate in regional peacekeeping operations. According to one account, at the start of the new millennium, the high prevalence of HIV in African armed forces hampered the United Nations' capacity to fulfill the demand for peacekeepers on the continent. The epidemic undermines peacekeeping capacity in three ways. First, HIV/AIDS is making states reluctant to contribute peacekeepers. One study found HIV prevalence among peacekeepers in Sierra Leone rose from 7% to 15% during a three-year deployment. Faced with the positive correlation between peacekeeping and HIV prevalence, African states are less willing to contribute forces to peacekeeping operations. Second, high HIV prevalence reduces the ability of African armed forces to deploy peacekeepers. The combination of a high HIV-prevalence among SANDF personnel and a policy of excluding HIV-positive troops from UN peacekeeping duty means that a significant portion of troops are unavailable for deployment. A 2003 RAND study reported that one South African official supposedly claimed that HIV/AIDS was the primary reason South Africa has not been more involved in the conflict in the Democratic Republic of the Congo.

Some have argued that even the perception of security vulnerability from infectious diseases could trigger opportunistic invasion.

Implications for US National Security

The specific effects and risks to a nation's military are unique to individual infectious diseases. However, the case of HIV/AIDS in African armed forces offers general insights into the potential effects of infectious diseases on the militaries of developing nations, with implications for the national security of Western countries, who have the capacity to help address some of these concerns.

Infectious diseases can threaten the domestic security and stability of developing nations where Western nations have significant national interest. Armed forces are often called upon to maintain domestic security. Militaries crippled by HIV/AIDS are less able to operate in this capacity. Governments unable to maintain domestic security could be perceived as less legitimate by the civilian population and increase popular support for non-state armed opposition groups. Thus, the demands placed on armed forces to protect against domestic threats would be likely negatively related to the military's own effectiveness.

Militaries of developing nations heavily burdened by infectious diseases are vulnerable to external threats. Regional stability is maintained by a balance of power. Shifts in the power dynamic among states increase the risk of interstate war. Militaries of developing nations weakened by infectious diseases are less able to deter international aggression. Some have argued that even the perception of security vulnerability from infectious diseases could trigger opportunistic invasion. Western nations have an interest in maintaining regional stability, not only for normative reasons, but also to protect strategic or economic national interests in the area.

Infectious diseases could limit a state's capacity to conduct peacekeeping operations. States with militaries debilitated by infectious diseases would be less able to muster an effective peacekeeping force from their reduced ranks. Even if a military had the capacity to contribute peacekeepers, the state might be reluctant to deploy them and stretch their already thinning ranks. Furthermore, states hosting peacekeeping forces could resist the presence of infected troops and the resultant risk of spreading the disease to their citizens. As infectious diseases reduce a state's peacekeeping capacity the burden could increasingly fall on the United States and its Western allies to maintain regional stability or risk wider conflicts.

Infectious Disease and US National Security Policy

In the 21st century, infectious diseases are increasingly a serious threat to global security. In particular, Western programmes to strengthen the effectiveness of developing world security forces must also increase their health capacity and the ability of friendly foreign armed forces to respond to infectious diseases within their ranks. The framework for such programmes already exists. The United States' African Contingency Operations Training and Assistance programme boosts the capacity of African militaries to conduct peacekeeping and humanitarian missions on the continent. Its greatest challenge, according to one commentator, is that the HIV/AIDS epidemic is crippling the participating militaries before they can be effectively deployed. Enlarging the role of health capacity building in this and similar programmes offers a means to make friendly militaries more resistant to infectious disease, increasing their ability to provide domestic, international, and regional stability.

The Ecology of Disease

Jim Robbins

Jim Robbins is a regular contributor to The New York Times's *science section.*

Breakdowns in ecosystems resulting from the development and destruction of the environment have unleashed most emerging infectious diseases and epidemics. Public health experts now factor ecology into their models, finding that the majority of pathogens spread to humans from wild and domestic animals is due to deforestation, urbanization, and agriculture. For instance, outbreaks of the closely related Nipah and Hendra viruses demonstrate how a harmless disease in bats can jump to vulnerable animals and humans; with Hendra, the outbreak was caused by suburbanization that attracted the bats to human habitats. Consequently, researchers and specialists monitor development of forests and rural areas to prevent or predict outbreaks.

There's a term biologists and economists use these days—ecosystem services—which refers to the many ways nature supports the human endeavor. Forests filter the water we drink, for example, and birds and bees pollinate crops, both of which have substantial economic as well as biological value.

If we fail to understand and take care of the natural world, it can cause a breakdown of these systems and come back to haunt us in ways we know little about. A critical example is a developing model of infectious disease that shows that most epidemics—AIDS, Ebola, West Nile, SARS, Lyme disease and hundreds more that have occurred over the last several decades—don't just happen. They are a result of things people do to nature.

Disease, it turns out, is largely an environmental issue. Sixty percent of emerging infectious diseases that affect humans are zoonotic—they originate in animals. And more than two-thirds of those originate in wildlife.

Teams of veterinarians and conservation biologists are in the midst of a global effort with medical doctors and epidemiologists to understand the "ecology of disease." It is part of a project called Predict, which is financed by the United States Agency for International Development. Experts are trying to figure out, based on how people alter the landscape—with a new farm or road, for example—where the next diseases are likely to spill over into humans and how to spot them when they do emerge, before they can spread. They are gathering blood, saliva and other samples from high-risk wildlife species to create a library of viruses so that if one does infect humans, it can be more quickly identified. And they are studying ways of managing forests, wildlife and livestock to prevent diseases from leaving the woods and becoming the next pandemic.

It isn't only a public health issue, but an economic one. The World Bank has estimated that a severe influenza pandemic, for example, could cost the world economy $3 trillion.

The problem is exacerbated by how livestock are kept in poor countries, which can magnify diseases borne by wild animals. A study released earlier this month by the International Livestock Research Institute found that more than two million people a year are killed by diseases that spread to humans from wild and domestic animals.

The Nipah virus in South Asia, and the closely related Hendra virus in Australia, both in the genus of henipah viruses, are the most urgent examples of how disrupting an ecosystem can cause disease. The viruses originated with flying foxes, Pteropus vampyrus, also known as fruit bats. They are messy eaters, no small matter in this scenario. They often hang upside down, looking like Dracula wrapped tightly in their membranous wings, and eat fruit by masticating the pulp and then spitting out the juices and seeds.

The bats have evolved with henipah over millions of years, and because of this co-evolution, they experience little more from it than the fruit bat equivalent of a cold. But once the virus breaks out of the bats and into species that haven't evolved with it, a horror show can occur, as one did in 1999 in rural Malaysia. It is likely that a bat dropped a piece of chewed fruit into a piggery in a forest. The pigs became infected with the virus, and amplified it, and it jumped to humans. It was startling in its lethality. Out of 276 people infected in Malaysia, 106 died, and many others suffered permanent and crippling neurological disorders. There is no cure or vaccine. Since then there have been 12 smaller outbreaks in South Asia.

In Australia, where four people and dozens of horses have died of Hendra, the scenario was different: suburbanization lured infected bats that were once forest-dwellers into backyards and pastures. If a henipah virus evolves to be transmitted readily through casual contact, the concern is that it could leave the jungle and spread throughout Asia or the world. "Nipah is spilling over, and we are observing these small clusters of cases—and it's a matter of time that the right strain will come along and efficiently spread among people," says Jonathan Epstein, a veterinarian with EcoHealth Alliance, a New York-based organization that studies the ecological causes of disease.

That's why experts say it's critical to understand underlying causes. "Any emerging disease in the last 30 or 40 years has come about as a result of encroachment into wild lands and changes in demography," says Peter Daszak, a disease ecologist and the president of EcoHealth.

Emerging infectious diseases are either new types of pathogens or old ones that have mutated to become novel, as the flu does every year. AIDS, for example, crossed into humans from chimpanzees in the 1920s when bush-meat hunters in Africa killed and butchered them.

Diseases have always come out of the woods and wildlife and found their way into human populations—the plague and malaria are two examples. But emerging diseases have quadrupled in the last half-century, experts say, largely because of increasing human encroachment into habitat, especially in disease "hot spots" around the globe, mostly in tropical regions. And with modern air travel and a robust market in wildlife trafficking, the potential for a serious outbreak in large population centers is enormous.

The key to forecasting and preventing the next pandemic, experts say, is understanding what they call the "protective effects" of nature intact. In the Amazon, for example, one study showed an increase in deforestation by some 4 percent increased the incidence of malaria by nearly 50 percent, because mosquitoes, which transmit the disease, thrive in the right mix of sunlight and water in recently deforested areas. Developing the forest in the wrong way can be like opening Pandora's box. These are the kinds of connections the new teams are unraveling.

Public health experts have begun to factor ecology into their models. Australia, for example, has just announced a multimillion-dollar effort to understand the ecology of the Hendra virus and bats.

It's not just the invasion of intact tropical landscapes that can cause disease. The West Nile virus came to the United States from Africa but spread here because one of its favored hosts is the American robin, which thrives in a world of lawns and agricultural fields. And mosquitoes, which spread the disease, find robins especially appealing. "The virus has had an important impact on human health in the United States because it took advantage of species that do well around people," says Marm Kilpatrick, a biologist at the University of California, Santa Cruz. The pivotal role of the robin in West Nile has earned it the title "super spreader."

And Lyme disease, the East Coast scourge, is very much a product of human changes to the environment: the reduction and fragmentation of large contiguous forests. Development chased off predators—wolves, foxes, owls and hawks. That has resulted in a fivefold increase in white-footed mice, which are great "reservoirs" for the Lyme bacteria, probably because they have poor immune systems. And they are terrible groomers. When possums or gray squirrels groom, they remove 90 percent of the larval ticks that spread the disease, while mice kill just half. "So mice are producing huge numbers of infected nymphs," says the Lyme disease researcher Richard Ostfeld.

"When we do things in an ecosystem that erode biodiversity—we chop forests into bits or replace habitat with agricultural fields—we tend to get rid of species that serve a protective role," Dr. Ostfeld told me. "There are a few species that are reservoirs and a lot of species that are not. The ones we encourage are the ones that play reservoir roles."

Dr. Ostfeld has seen two emerging diseases—babesiosis and anaplasmosis—that affect humans in the ticks he studies, and he has raised the alarm about the possibility of their spread.

The best way to prevent the next outbreak in humans, specialists say, is with what they call the One Health Initiative—a worldwide program, involving more than 600 scientists and other professionals, that advances the idea that human, animal and ecological health are inextricably linked and need to be studied and managed holistically.

"It's not about keeping pristine forest pristine and free of people," says Simon Anthony, a molecular virologist at the Center for Infection and Immunity at Columbia University's Mailman School of Public Health. "It's learning how to do things sustainably. If you can get a handle on what it is that drives the emergence of a disease, then you can learn to modify environments sustainably."

The scope of the problem is huge and complex. Just an estimated 1 percent of wildlife viruses are known. Another major factor is the immunology of wildlife, a science in its infancy. Raina K. Plowright, a biologist at Pennsylvania State University who studies the ecology of disease, found that outbreaks of the Hendra virus in flying foxes in rural areas were rare but were much higher in urban and suburban animals. She hypothesizes that urbanized bats are sedentary and miss the frequent exposure to the virus they used to get in the wild, which kept the infection at low levels. That means more bats—whether from poor nutrition, loss of habitat or other factors—become infected and shed more of the virus into backyards.

The fate of the next pandemic may be riding on the work of Predict. EcoHealth and its partners—the University of California at Davis, the Wildlife Conservation Society, the Smithsonian Institution and Global Viral Forecasting—are looking at wildlife-borne viruses across the tropics, building a virus library. Most of the work focuses on primates, rats and bats, which are most likely to carry diseases that affect people.

Most critically, researchers are watching the interface where deadly viruses are known to exist and where people are breaking open the forest, as they are along the new highway from the Atlantic to the Pacific across the Andes in Brazil and Peru. "By mapping encroachment into the forest you can predict where the next disease could emerge," Dr. Daszak, EcoHealth's president, says. "So we're going to the edge of villages, we're going to places where mines have just opened up, areas where new roads are being built. We are going to talk to people who live within these zones and saying, 'what you are doing is potentially a risk.'"

It might mean talking to people about how they butcher and eat bush meat or to those who are building a feed lot in bat habitat. In Bangladesh, where Nipah broke out several times, the disease was traced to bats that were raiding containers that collected date palm sap, which people drank. The disease source was eliminated by placing bamboo screens (which cost 8 cents each) over the collectors.

EcoHealth also scans luggage and packages at airports, looking for imported wildlife likely to be carrying deadly viruses. And they have a program called PetWatch to warn consumers about exotic pets that are pulled out of the forest in disease hot spots and shipped to market.

All in all, the knowledge gained in the last couple of years about emerging diseases should allow us to sleep a little easier, says Dr. Epstein, the EcoHealth veterinarian. "For the first time," he said, "there is a coordinated effort in 20 countries to develop an early warning system for emerging zoonotic outbreaks."

4

Fears of Infectious Diseases Are Based on Racism

Stanley M. Aronson

Stanley M. Aronson is founding dean of the medical school at Brown University.

Although humans have never lived free of bacteria or viruses, deadly and fearsome communicable diseases—from the Spanish flu to Ebola fever—always seem to arrive from Africa, Asia, or other lands far off from America. While seemingly harmless, these racist names divide the world into the contaminated and uncontaminated, blaming and creating fear of developing countries and ethnicities for emerging infections and pandemics. Furthermore, rather than being disease-free, the United States has faced dozens of new and resurgent human pathogens over the past four decades; in fact, the 1918 influenza pandemic attributed to the Spanish flu actually originated in Kansas.

We humans have never lived in a bacterially sterile world, a world free of disease-causing germs. Nor dare we envision a future time when infectious disease will have retreated to history books lest we join those past civilizations that relied solely on fanciful illusions.

During the last millennium there have been three lethal pandemics, killing millions of souls. The great bubonic plague commencing in 1346, sometimes called the Black Death, altered the economy of 14th Century Europe, presaging the end

Stanley M. Aronson, "Racism and the Threat of Influenza," *Medicine & Health Rhode Island*, vol. 93, no.1, January 2010, p. 3. Copyright © 2010 Medicine & Health Rhode Island. All rights reserved. Reproduced by permission.

of its feudal economy and witnessing the hesitant beginnings of more diversified farming, and in cities, cottage industries. The plague killed perhaps one fourth of the European population.

The second communicable disease tragedy was the awesome influenza pandemic commencing in the summer of 1918 and killing in excess of 50 million people within 18 months. And we are in the midst of a third global pestilence, AIDS.

How, in general terms, do communicable disease threats, such as influenza, arise? Are they merely random phenomena, part of what mathematicians call chaos theory and hence unpredictable? Are they, perhaps, capricious happenings, proof of humanity's maladaptive status in the overall scheme of things and therefore both tragedies and warnings that we repent? Are they, alternatively, manifestations of divine punishment, the predominant belief until the last century? Or, perhaps, are there underlying trends, secular patterns, etiological relationships in these various pestilences which, with more careful scrutiny, serve to clarify the dynamics and origins of pandemics?

And why, parenthetically, do these global perils always seem to take origin in distant, exotic places? We hear of Spanish flu, Asian flu, Hong Kong flu, Ebola fever, Lassa fever, tsutsugamushi, Siberian tick fever. But almost never do we hear of Jersey City influenza, Barrington encephalitis or Woonsocket fever.

Underlying this innocent perception of the contaminated and uncontaminated segments of the world . . . rests a subtle form of racism which simplistically divides the world by ethnicity.

And we who are privileged to give geographic names to newly encountered pestilences live under the naïve impression that we Americans prosper in an idyllic, pestilence-free community; and were it not for those alien pathogens from distant, unclean communities such as rain forests with strange names, we would thrive in a contagion-free society. Why, Oh why, said Henry Higgins [a character in the play *Pygmalion* and the musical *My Fair Lady*], can't the rest of the world be just like us?

Hyperbole perhaps, yet our American society truly contends that through clean living—and some marginal help from medical science—we have arrived at what the Pilgrims had called that shining city on the hill, essentially free of nasty pestilences.

Between "Them" and "Us"

Underlying this innocent perception of the contaminated and uncontaminated segments of the world, between the "them" (the teeming masses infested with communicable disease) and the "us", essentially disease-free but now needlessly threatened by the unclean world beyond our borders, rests a subtle form of racism which simplistically divides the world by ethnicity and is prompted by the inchoate fear that the third world is intent on sending both its uneducated young and its threatening pathogens to seek shelter on our pristine shores. It is the 21st Century variant of [newspaper owner William Randolph] Hearst's 19th Century Yellow Peril [a racist metaphor for Asian immigrants].

It is an old tradition to assign blame before seeking constructive explanations. What person, tradition or institution can we blame for the unremitting threat of influenza? Epidemiologists, tracing the origins of new pandemics, tell us that China's vast population of humans living in close proximity with two billion swine and ten billion domesticated poultry has generated many of the past influenza pandemics—and will likely do so again in the future. The biological crucible for mixing human, avian and swine influenza genes is there, and for reasons other than malice, China is therefore the likeliest location for a new and communicable influenza virus to be generated, emerging into the neighboring human population and then spreading to the other continents.

In truth, since 1974, this nation has been challenged by 29 new or resurgent human pathogens including HIV infection (AIDS), Lyme disease, legionnaire's disease, cryptosporidiosis, SARS [severe acute respiratory syndrome], avian flu, swine flu and more than a score of others; most, but not all, originating from less developed regions of the globe.

But it is well to recall, lest we think that the United States is a virologically privileged territory without its share of inciting world pandemics of influenza, that the tragic 1918 influenza pandemic, inaccurately called the Spanish flu and still the most lethal pestilence in human history, originated in the American prairies of Haskell County, Kansas.

5

Eradicating Infectious Diseases Could Have Unintended Consequences

Natalie Wolchover

Natalie Wolchover is a staff writer for Life's Little Mysteries, a website that investigates a variety of scientific, environmental, and social topics.

Ridding the world of HIV, malaria, the flu, and other infectious diseases would neither be universally beneficial nor cause the downfall of humanity. While human evolution has benefitted from the presence of pathogens, their absence today—as seen with the eradication of malaria in the United States—poses only minimal risks. Moreover, while the eradication of infectious diseases would result in significant population growth, the world's social and economic problems would be much more manageable without them. Uncertainties regarding human health arise, however, as some viruses may play a role in human growth and development, and the use of antibiotics has eliminated good bacteria along with the bad, resulting in autoimmune diseases.

Imagine a world with no HIV, no malaria, no tuberculosis, no flu and so on down to the absence of the common cold. With scientists chasing after cure-all anti-virus treatments and a universal flu vaccine in labs around the world, the eradication of infectious diseases certainly appears to be medical research's ultimate (if remote) goal. But what if we actually got there?

As the Princeton mathematical epidemiologist Nim Arinaminpathy put it, "If we had a magic pill that got rid of all infectious diseases, period, would we really use it?" He isn't sure. In all likelihood, purging humanity of infectious disease would not be a universally positive eventuality, but it wouldn't trigger the immediate downfall of *Homo sapiens*, either.

Survival of the Unfittest

First, consider what we'd be giving up. "Our evolutionary history has been a continual arms race against the pathogens that plague us," said Vincent Racaniello, professor of microbiology and immunology at Columbia University. For eons, this battle has weeded out the weak, and in a less combative environment, standards for human survival would grow lax.

However, this is not quite as problematic as it might seem. In much of the West, "people are already kind of artificial animals," Racaniello told Life's Little Mysteries. "We have all these ways of intervening when people get sick, when otherwise they would have died and we would see some natural selection for people with more robust immune systems." But as long as doctors keep having a way to render moot those diseases that used to kill us, natural immunity isn't essential, he said.

And in fact, many diseases could be eradicated worldwide without any loss of evolutionary robustness. "With influenza, there isn't any indication that this plays a role in human evolution," said Arinaminpathy, who studies the evolutionary effects of flu vaccines. A pathogen can only impact human DNA if it tends to kill people before they have offspring. Otherwise, its victims have already passed on their genes to the next generation, regardless of whether those genes made them susceptible to the pathogen or not. The flu is most fatal to the elderly, who have typically already passed on their genes.

Meanwhile, malaria does target the young, and it therefore molds the evolution of people in many tropical countries by killing children with feeble immune defenses (leaving behind those with malaria-resistant genes). But this "survival of the fittest" situation is not desirable; malaria has been largely eradicated in the United States with no obvious downsides. If the same were to happen in Africa and other afflicted regions, "the impact of reducing or removing malaria would go beyond public health," Arinaminpathy said.

A Healthy Population

The malaria parasite is so rampant in Africa that many children are afflicted over and over in a nearly continuous cycle. "You can't think clearly, you feel terrible, and it stops you from being able to go to school or have a productive life," Racaniello said. Meanwhile, HIV is running amok in sub-Saharan Africa, similarly stifling development and productivity.

In short, disease ushers in poverty. "If you get rid of infectious diseases by vaccination," Racaniello said, "you can make a big contribution to getting people out of poverty so they can have productive lives."

And although wiping out malaria, tuberculosis, sleeping sickness, HIV and the other tropical plagues would mean significant population growth in just the areas that are already experiencing runaway birth rates and food crises, these socioeconomic problems would be far more tractable in a disease-free society. "If a good fraction of these individuals have productive careers they might come up with solutions," he said.

Would a world in which babies were permanently inoculated against the cold, the flu, HPV and everything else actually be better?

These considerations all suggest eradicating infectious diseases would benefit humanity, on balance. But there's one giant question left.

Good Colds?

Does regularly getting the cold or the flu when we're young help us later? These viruses might somehow aid in the growth and development of our metabolisms, or even our organs. Scientists aren't sure, because they haven't had the chance to study a virus-free human population, as they have with the bacteria- and parasite-lacking populations in the West.

"We're just learning that the consequence of antibiotics is that when you get rid of the good bacteria in our guts, we can develop autoimmune diseases [such as allergies]. We're not as advanced in our understanding of viruses. What do viruses do for us?" Racaniello said.

Allergies we can live with, but some of the benign viruses that hitch a ride in our bodies could be serving a much deeper role, Arinaminpathy said—as could a few of the slightly virulent ones with whom our relationship is "a bit fuzzy." Would a world in which babies were permanently inoculated against the cold, the flu, HPV [human papillomavirus] and everything else actually be better?

Like always, we should be careful what we wish for. Ridding the world of diseases would be "mostly a good thing," Arinaminpathy said, "but there are these interesting questions when you scratch the surface of these illnesses."

6

The Path of a Pandemic

Laurie Garrett

A Pulitzer Prize–winning journalist, Laurie Garrett is the author of The Coming Plague: Newly Emerging Diseases in a World Out of Balance *and is the senior fellow for global health at the Council on Foreign Relations.*

Strains of influenza that jump from animals to humans are a growing threat. Globalization and ecological changes caused by humans dramatically increase opportunities for the flu virus to evolve, mutate, and spread. In recent years, emerging infections were caused by combinations of pig, bird, and human flu that acquired new genetic material over time. At present, the world has a new H1N1 virus that does not respond to one type of anti-flu drug, and its deadliness and path remain unknown. A related virus is also in circulation, which could reassort with the new virus and become one with even more drug resistance. Finally, there is H5N1, an older virus that is less lethal but more easily transmitted. If action is not taken, the ecology promoting the spread and evolution of the virus may lead to the deadliest flu pandemic yet.

*H*ow one virus spread from pigs and birds to humans around the globe. And why microbes like H1N1 flu have become a growing threat.

Around Thanksgiving 2005 a teenage boy helped his brother-in-law butcher 31 pigs at a local Wisconsin slaughterhouse, and a week later the 17-year-old pinned down another pig while it was gutted. In the lead-up to the holidays the boy's family bought a chicken and kept the animal in their home, out of the harsh Sheboygan autumn. On Dec. 7, the teenager came down with the flu, suffering an illness that lasted three days. He visited a local clinic, then fully recovered, and nobody else in his family took ill.

This incident would hardly seem worth mentioning except that the influenza virus that infected the Wisconsin lad was unlike any previously seen. It appeared to be a mosaic of a wild-bird form of flu, a human type and a strain found in pigs.

It was an H1N1 swine influenza. Largely ignored at the time, the Wisconsin virus was a step along the evolutionary tree, leading to a virus that four years later would stun the world.

Flash-forward to April 2009, and young Edgar Enrique Hernandez in faraway La Gloria, Mexico, suffers a bout of flu, found to be caused by a similar mosaic of swine/bird/human flu, also H1N1. And thousands of miles away in Cairo, the Egyptian government decides pigs are the source of disease, and orders 300,000 animals in the predominantly Muslim (therefore not pork-consuming) society slaughtered.

Each of these three incidents is related to the unfolding influenza crisis. It is the manner of human beings to seek blame during times of fear. Fingers are now pointing, either at the entire pig species *Sus domestica*, or at the nation of Mexico. Such exercises in blame are not only scientifically ill founded but are likely to prompt government actions that, at the very least, are useless and, at worst, harmful for efforts to control a pandemic.

We live in a globalized world, filled with shared microbial threats that arise in one place, are amplified somewhere else through human activities that aid and abet the germs, and then traverse vast geographic terrains in days, even hours— again, thanks to human activities and movements. If there is blame to be meted out, it should be directed at the species Homo sapiens and the manifest ways in which we are reshaping the world ecology, offering germs like the influenza virus extraordinary new opportunities to evolve, mutate and spread.

Back in 2005, the Wisconsin Division of Public Health hunted for sick pigs in Sheboygan County, but the animals the teenager had helped slaughter came from multiple farms across the area, and every farmer claimed his herd was healthy. The Wisconsin authorities forwarded blood samples from the infected teenager and his family to the Centers for Disease Control and Prevention in Atlanta. The CDC scientists discovered that the H1N1 virus had pieces of its RNA genetic material that matched a human flu first seen in New Caledonia in 1999, two swine types that had been circulating in Asia and Wisconsin for several years and an unknown avian-flu virus.

In 2006 the American Association of Swine Veterinarians reported that humans were passing their H1N1 viruses to pigs, causing widespread illness in swine herds, especially in the American Midwest. A year later at a county fair in Ohio an outbreak occurred, sickening many of the pigs, but not their human handlers. The cause was a type of H1N1 that was a close match to the Wisconsin strain, and may have been spread from human to pig.

Last year researchers from Iowa State University in Ames warned that pigs located in industrial-scale farms were being subjected to influenza infections from farm poultry, wild birds and their human handlers. Writing in *The Journal of Infectious Diseases*, Eileen Thacker and Bruce Janke said, "As a result of the constantly changing genetic makeup of individual influenza viruses in pigs, the U.S. swine industry is continually scrambling to respond to the influenza viruses circulating within individual production systems."

Something was changing. Pigs notoriously eat just about anything thrown their way, and rub up against each other frequently, readily passing infections within herds. Their stomachs are remarkably tolerant environs for microbes, which since ancient times have caused illness in humans who dined on raw or undercooked pork. Investigation of the 1918 influenza pandemic, which is now estimated to have killed up to 100 million people worldwide in 18 months, revealed that the viral culprit was a type H1N1 human flu that had infected pigs, and then circulated back to humans.

At the viral level, influenza is an awfully sloppy microbe that is in a constant state of mutation and evolution. Its genetic material is in the form of RNA (not DNA, as in humans), loosely collected into chromosomes. When a virus infects a cell, its chromosomes essentially fall apart into a mess, which is copied to make more viruses that then enter the bloodstream to spread throughout the body. Along the way in this copying process any other genetic material that may be lying about the cell is also stuffed into the thousands of viral copies that are made. If the virus happens to be reproducing this way inside a human cell, it picks up *Homo sapiens* genetic material; from a chicken cell it absorbs avian genes; and from a pig cell it garners swine RNA. The jackpot events in influenza evolution occur when two different types of flu viruses happen to get into an animal cell at the same time, swapping entire chromosomes to create "reassorted" viruses.

What was infecting that teenager in Sheboygan was a triple reassortment, resulting in a new virus with bits of genes from three species of animals—one of them *Homo sapiens.*

But who pays attention to such things? Other than vets, pig farmers and the occasional virologist, not many people in public health, government or medicine usually give much thought to the four-legged viral mixing vessels that oink their way around family farms and vast industrial pork-production centers. Thacker and Janke's 2008 writing seems sadly prescient today: "Pigs would be an ideal mixing vessel for the creation of new avian/mammalian influenza viruses capable of causing novel diseases with the potential for producing pandemics in the human population—It is apparent that, in the U.S. swine industry, transmission of influenza viruses between swine and humans is fairly common and is bidirectional."

Nine months ago the Texas Department of State Health Services reported the case to the CDC of an individual who was exposed to ailing pigs. The Texan came down with flu, spread it to no one and was fine after a few days. In the patient's blood, CDC scientists found "a swine influenza A (H1N1) triple reassortant virus, A/Wisconsin/87/2005 H1N1," the same virus that infected the Sheboygan teenager three years earlier.

And then, this March, the outbreak of 2009 commenced. It might not have been noticed, frankly, if things unfolded in the same bird/human/swine manner as had previously evoked only humdrum attention in Wisconsin, Ohio and Texas. But this time, people died.

In mid-March the number of routinely reported influenza cases in several Mexican states suddenly spiked upward. At roughly the same time, public-health authorities in southern California spotted two separate cases of flu in children: a 10-year-old boy in San Diego County, and a 9-year-old girl in Imperial County. Though both children survived their illnesses, there was evidence that it had spread to family members, and samples of the children's blood were examined at the CDC in early April. Bingo: H1N1 triple-reassorted influenza. Meanwhile, in Mexico, more than 50 serious flu cases emerged over the same time period, and the government forwarded blood samples to Canada's top infectious-diseases lab in Winnipeg. The Canadians confirmed that the Mexican mystery virus was H1N1, and the potential pandemic saga unfolded.

In Mexico, attention has focused on little Edgar Enrique Hernandez, who is believed to have come down with the new flu on April 2. The blame for Hernandez's infection is aimed at an American-owned industrial pig center located near the child's home in La Gloria. Residents had long complained about the stench and dust from the plant, and have eagerly named it as the source of the child's infection. It may be true that Hernandez inhaled H1N1 from a pig, but because other cases emerged in March, the timing of the case is off: Edgar Hernandez is not Patient Zero in the outbreak of 2009.

This virus has been evolving for a long time, no doubt aided in its transformation by the ecology of industrial-scale pig farming in North America. Some scientists say there are genetic elements in the virus that date back to an Indiana pig farm in 1987. In that sense, it is similar to the "bird flu," or H5N1, which surfaced in wild migratory water birds in southern China some time in the early 1990s and infected people in Hong Kong in 1997. As that virus has evolved over the past 12 years, it has taken advantage of large poultry farms, and major bird-migration centers, to spread rapidly and absorb new genetic material along the way. In 2005, as H5N1 spread to Siberia and Europe, the United Nations and the Bush administration mobilized cash, scientific expertise and the needed infrastructure to find and contain outbreaks, primarily by slaughtering infected chicken flocks.

In Indonesia, where the virus has spread to pigs and humans, it appears H5N1 can be passed, in rare cases, between people, and human infection is an extraordinarily dangerous event: 82 percent of infected Indonesians have succumbed to the flu virus. The global average mortality rate for H5N1 in people is 63 percent, which makes it one of the most fearsome microbes on earth.

Here, then, is where we stand.

We have a new virus in the world that appears to be very contagious between people, and possibly between swine and humans. It is, fortunately, treatable with the antiviral drugs Tamiflu and Relenza (oseltamivir and zanamivir), but it is resistant to the other major class of anti-flu drugs, amantadines. It is still evolving, and moving, and its ultimate trajectory cannot be seen right now. We do not yet know how deadly this virus is: while Mexico has been able to track down the numbers of dead and hospitalized H1N1 cases, it cannot determine just how many Mexicans have been infected with the virus since it started spreading there in late March. It's one thing to say that 150 people out of, perhaps, 10 million infected have died: that gives you a case fatality rate that is roughly what we see with normal, seasonal flu. (Each year, seasonal flu kills 36,000 people in the United States alone.) It's quite another story if Mexico's denominator is 5,000, for a case fatality rate of 3 percent—a full percentage point worse than the rate seen with the 1918 influenza. It is urgent that we discern the denominator.

We have a second, closely related H1N1 human virus in circulation around the world. Though widespread, it is not unusually lethal. Last year this virus developed full resistance to Tamiflu. It would be most disturbing if the 2008 H1N1 human virus were to reassort with the new swine/human virus, as we could then be facing a more drug-resistant pandemic strain of influenza, treatable only with the drug Relenza, which must be administered with an inhaler device.

We have a third, older pandemic in poultry, occasionally infecting humans, that involves the H5N1 virus. This pandemic has circulated long enough so that the virus has branched into several evolutionary trees, including forms that are drug-resistant. In Egypt, where it is common for urban families to raise chickens in their yards, H5N1 has caused a significant number of human cases, and its spread appears to be uncontrolled. The World Health Organization (WHO) is distressed by evidence that H5N1 is becoming less deadly for people. That could mean that the bird-flu virus is evolving toward a less-lethal form that is more capable of spreading between people.

It is supremely ironic, then, that the Egyptian government in late April started slaughtering the nation's 300,000 pigs as an alleged flu-control measure. The swine form of H1N1 may not be in Egypt as of this writing, but the chicken H5N1 most definitely is, and has to date infected 68 Egyptians, killing 23. Egypt has never carried out wholesale slaughter of poultry, as chicken is a staple of the national diet. Pork, in contrast, is consumed only by the minority Christian population. An Egyptian Islamist group has declared that swine flu is "God's revenge against infidels."

The Muslim Brotherhood in Egypt recently declared that the Cairo-based U.S. Naval Medical Research Unit (NAMRU), which has provided public-health work for the entire Middle East for decades, must be shut down, and Egypt must stop sending samples of H5N1 viruses that emerge in the country to the WHO. The Egyptian group, which holds seats in Parliament, is echoing sentiments first put forward by Indonesia's minister of health, Siti Supari, who has refused to share her country's H5N1 samples with the WHO since 2006. Supari is also trying to evict another NAMRU lab from Jakarta. On April 28, Supari declared that the new swine flu was genetically engineered and released in order to promote American pharmaceutical sales worldwide.

Two days later, Supari denied making such statements, though they were consistent with her longstanding claim that rich countries—particularly the United States—prey on poorer nations in the interest of drug-company profits. In heated negotiations with the World Health Organization and the U.S. government, Supari has insisted on the existence of "viral sovereignty," wherein nations own any viruses that they discover within their boundaries, have the right to refuse sharing them with the WHO or any other foreign entity and may demand all profits derived from vaccines and other products made from those viruses. Under this principle, Indonesia refuses to allow the outside world access to at least 50 H5N1 strains thought to have emerged in that country since 2005. Without access to the various viral strains, scientists cannot tell if

H5N1 is evolving dangerous attributes in Indonesia, or whether the hideously high death rate in infected people there is due to some unique viral characteristics. Therefore, the principle of viral sovereignty directly imperils the entire global community—as well as Supari's own people. On April 30, the WHO repudiated another Supari claim: that Indonesians have special genetic or environmental traits that would keep them safe from the new swine flu.

Happily, Mexico has shown the world how a responsible nation can respond to a potential pandemic. By moving swiftly to shut down schools, entertainment and places of social congregation, Mexico—an already beleaguered economy—is facing dire financial consequences. But its dramatic actions may be saving Mexican lives, and slowing down the outbreak of 2009. In that sense, the world owes Mexico a big gracias.

Governments the world over would do well to pay attention to Mexico's response, and learn from it. Throughout Asia, governments have been pulling their old SARS-epidemic thermal monitors out of mothballs, and scanning people for evidence of fevers. That worked for SARS control because the SARS virus was almost exclusively contagious when people were running fevers. Not so with influenza: flu can be very contagious before the individual carrier has any symptoms at all, much less a fever.

Worse, some governments are banning pork products from the Americas, as if it were possible to get the flu from eating a cooked sausage. It is not.

A wiser set of pig-related actions would turn to the strange ecology we have created to feed meat to our massive human population. It is a strange world wherein billions of animals are concentrated into tiny spaces, breeding stock is flown to production sites all over the world and poorly paid migrant workers are exposed to infected animals. And it's going to get much worse, as the world's once poor populations of India and China enter the middle class. Back in 1980 the per capita meat consumption in China was about 44 pounds a year: it now tops 110 pounds. In 1983 the world consumed 152 million tons of meat a year. By 1997 consumption was up to 233 million tons. And the United Nations Food and Agriculture Organization estimates that by 2020 world consumption could top 386 million tons of pork, chicken, beef and farmed fish.

This is the ecology that, in the cases of pigs and chickens, is breeding influenza. It is an ecology that promotes viral evolution. And if we don't do something about it, this ecology will one day spawn a severe pandemic that will dwarf that of 1918.

7

Fears of an Influenza Pandemic Are Overblown

Kathryn Blaze Carlson

Kathryn Blaze Carlson is a writer for the National Post, *a Canadian newspaper.*

A recent strain of the influenza virus H1N1 is a cause for concern. But it is treatable with accessible drugs, effectively vaccinated against, and far less deadly than the seasonal flu. Nonetheless, fears of it spread rapidly, inflamed by global health experts and organizations. In fact, the virus has been touted as a threat to national security and compared to the devastating 1918 Spanish flu. This reflects a worst-case mentality among officials, who emphasize the contagiousness and danger of H1N1 without considering impressions on the public. And some observers speculate that these fears reflect another fear—of underestimating or underpreparing for a flu outbreak—and opportunism on the part of the health and pharmaceutical industries.

It was just six months ago that the U.S. Centers for Disease Control and Prevention reported that two children in California had developed a respiratory illness never before seen in humans, referring to the infection as "swine flu" in its Morbidity and Mortality Weekly Report.

That was on April 21 [2009]. By May 1, the government of Egypt had slaughtered all of the country's 300,000 pigs, despite the fact not a single case of the virus had struck the nation. It was not long before major markets such as China and Russia blocked pork imports and family's scratched ham off their grocery lists, even though the virus cannot be contracted by consuming properly cooked pork.

A month after declaring that "the whole of humanity is under threat," the head of the World Health Organization announced that H1N1 influenza had reached the pandemic phase, marking the first official global flu pandemic in 41 years. By July, Britain's Department of Health had recommended that women should "consider delaying conception whilst the pandemic is going on."

Around the world, school closures were ordered, churches were advised to drain their holy-water basins, hand-sanitizer sales have surged, and travellers fled the beaches of Mexico, where the H1N1 virus claimed its first victims.

"We must all be deeply concerned about the impact that even a moderate pandemic will have on vulnerable populations," said Margaret Chan, director-general of the WHO during a speech delivered in June.

Much of the language surrounding the flu is inflammatory and does little more than instil a paralyzing paranoia among a species already programmed for fight or flight and which increasingly views any uncertainty as a threat.

Fear Spreading Ferociously

To be sure, the H1N1 virus is cause for concern. It has appeared in 191 countries, struck roughly 400,000 people globally and claimed the lives of at least 5,000 people. However the virus, a novel strain of influenza that can be treated with two widely available drugs and for which there is an effective vaccine, has killed fewer people over the past six months than the seasonal flu kills every six days. Yet fear of the flu has spread ferociously, as if H1N1 anxiety were more contagious than the virus itself.

"It appears that the global health community, including the WHO, is committed to worst-case thinking," said Frank Furedi, professor of Sociology at the University of Kent and author of *Politics of Fear, Where Have All the Intellectuals Gone?* "Health officials are today framing medical problems like H1N1 as threats to human existence."

For Mr. Ferudi, much of the language surrounding the flu is inflammatory and does little more than instil a paralyzing paranoia among a species already programmed for fight or flight and which increasingly views any uncertainty as a threat. Fear, of course, can be a positive emotion that protects people from taking dangerous risks, and is partly credited for humankind's early abilities to survive. But fear can likewise manifest into debilitating paranoia, and prevent people from engaging healthily in society.

"Emphasizing possibilities rather than probabilities can cause alarm," Mr. Ferudi said. "Health has been thrown into the current obsession with safety and security. It's a case of joined-up scare-mongering."

Indeed, in a twist from the traditional narrative, the H1N1 pandemic has been recast as a national security issue. In the WHO's 17th Pandemic 2009 Update, issued on Oct. 11, the organization said: "Systemic surveillance conducted by the Global Influenza Surveillance Network, continues to detect sporadic incidents of H1N1 pandemic viruses that show resistance to the antiviral oseltamivir."

Meantime, after a militant Egyptian Islamist group declared that H1N1 was "God's revenge against infidels," political pundits were quick to surmise that the virus could be deployed as an act of terrorism.

In a more subtle, but all the while security-framed tone, the U.K.'s Institute for Public Policy Research published a statement in August that said: "Over the past few months, the nature of the new security challenges we face has been highlighted by the rapid global spread of the swine flu pandemic. Experts have warned that several million people across the U.K. may be affected, with some predicting that in a worst-case scenario, as many as one in 200 people who contract the disease may die.... A more broadly based, joined-up and inclusive national security strategy is needed."

By referencing the Spanish Flu as a model for what might occur, health professionals ignore the modern health systems of most Western countries.

Since the first outbreak in the spring, health officials, medical journals and the media have repeatedly pointed to the 1918 Spanish Flu, which killed 50 million globally, as an example of the kind of havoc this new strain of influenza could wreak. This, Mr. Ferudi said, only serves to "transform the flu into an apocalyptic threat."

Worst-Case Mentality

It is not the scientific comparison of the H1N1 virus to the Spanish Flu—which was a subtype of the H1N1 strain—that seems to perturb Mr. Ferudi, but rather the manner in which the discussion is framed.

"By referencing the Spanish Flu as a model for what might occur, health professionals ignore the modern health systems of most Western countries."

Dan Epstein, spokesman for the WHO's Americas office, said that while the organization is cautious of the tone in its announcements, it does not consider people's psyche in determining whether a situation should be declared an outbreak, epidemic or pandemic. Instead, officials emphasize the transmissibility and threat posed by a given virus.

"The urgency in this instance was the increased number of cases and the very fact that this was a completely new virus that had never been seen before," he said. "We don't know what it can do."

[The threat of a pandemic] presents an opportunity for health officials and pharmaceutical companies to cash in people's fear for the sake of political and economic gain.

Some onlookers argue that it is the fear experienced by bureaucrats themselves—the fear of underestimating or underpreparing for a situation, much in the vein of Hurricane Katrina—that drives this sort of worst-case mentality.

In 2005, the United Nations "flu czar" frightened the world when he announced that the Avian Flu could kill as many as 150 million people worldwide. The threat never materialized, but Mr. Epstein said the Avian Flu experience nonetheless led to years spent "beefing up" pandemic preparation plans.

This, some charge, presents an opportunity for health officials and pharmaceutical companies to cash in people's fear for the sake of political and economic gain.

Ms. Chan, the director-general of the WHO, raised the eyebrows of skeptics across the globe when, on June 11, she said: "The world can now reap the benefits of investments over the last five years in pandemic preparedness."

But Andre Leroux, CEO [chief executive officer] of medical-supply company Noveko International, was unprepared for the fury that has ensued since that April day.

Roughly 100 million of the company's anti-microbial masks are currently on backorder, and 20,000 litres of hand-sanitizer are being sold each and every day—that is roughly the amount sold by the company in an average year.

"Our challenge is not sales, it's keeping up with demand," Mr. Leroux said.

"There's certainly a paranoia right now. People are definitely more conscious of the notion of clean air, it's part of the psyche now."

8

Global Health: Preparing for the Worst

The Economist

Based in London, The Economist *is a weekly news and international affairs magazine.*

Vaccine makers are not ready for an influenza pandemic. Different strains of influenza are active at any given time and evolve at varying paces, complicating vaccine development. Also, the production of flu vaccines currently involves egg-based manufacturing, a method that cannot quickly respond to a global pandemic. Posing additional risks, switching vaccine production from one strain to another may not protect against a following wave of a deadly strain. Innovations in manufacturing such as the use of cell cultures and adjuvants to improve efficacy and cut the amount of required active ingredients have potential, but these techniques have not yet been perfected or approved.

Vaccine makers are ill-prepared for an influenza epidemic.

Mexico City sprang back to life this week after two weeks of fear and inactivity. Officials shut down most of the economy to halt the spread of a previously unknown strain of the mongrel H1N1 virus, which is comprised of avian, swine and human influenza viruses. The hope is that the outbreak has now peaked.

If so, that will come as a relief to many, as the virus has spread rapidly around the world. On May 6th the World Health Organisation (WHO) reported 822 confirmed cases in Mexico, including 29 deaths. Altogether, 403 cases have been detected in the United States, including at least one death. Dozens of non-lethal cases have been found in 22 other countries. If a cluster of self-sustaining cases in a region outside the Americas is confirmed, the WHO will raise its concern from level five to the top of its six-level scale for global pandemics.

Richard Besser, the acting director of America's Centres for Disease Control (CDC), said the virus "so far is not looking more severe than a strain that we would see in seasonal flu." That is not as reassuring as it sounds. An influenza outbreak in 1918 began in a mild way, but returned in a lethal form months later and killed millions. Margaret Chan, the WHO's boss, cautioned: "it may come back . . . the world should prepare for it."

One of the best ways to do so is vaccination. Surveillance systems and antiviral treatments will help contain a disease, but they cannot halt it the way a vaccine could. Such a treatment would have to come from the makers of vaccines for the more ordinary, seasonal strains of flu. Yet despite all the advances in biological science, this industry still relies on capital-intensive, inflexible and old-fashioned technologies, such as producing vaccines from millions of chicken eggs.

The Drift and Shift

The production of flu vaccine has developed to cope with seasonal flu. The disease may seem no more than a nuisance to many, but the flu still kills perhaps 500,000 people a year around the world. It is hard to develop a perfect vaccine against seasonal influenza because it is so fleet-footed. There are usually several different strains of influenza active at any time, and these variations evolve. Alan Barrett of the University of Texas says travel by carriers of influenza, be they people in aeroplanes or birds on the wing, means regional mutations quickly spread around the world. Hence, even when flu subsides at the end of the northern hemisphere's winter, the disease merely shifts to the southern hemisphere (which is now entering its winter). Six months later, it moves back. When the mutations are gradual, as with seasonal flu, it is known as drift; when they are abrupt, as with the new strain of H1N1, you have a shift on your hands.

There's much greater vaccine capacity than there was a few years ago, but there is not enough vaccine capacity to instantly make vaccines for the entire world's population for influenza.

To help the vaccine manufacturers plan, the WHO issues guidelines every six months listing the three strains of seasonal flu that appear to pose the biggest threat during the relevant hemisphere's approaching winter. The firms then prepare their genetic cocktails and develop them inside live chicken eggs in sterile conditions. The resulting "trivalent" vaccine provokes the patient's immune system into producing antibodies, and that primes it for an attack by the worrying strains of flu.

The final product comes in two forms. Most of the world's flu vaccine is a killed virus, given as an injection; Europe's Sanofi Pasteur and Novartis are leading producers that use this approach. America's MedImmune has come up with a nasal spray that uses a live flu virus in a weakened form. Both methods use lots of eggs.

If a global pandemic is declared and manufacturers are asked to produce a vaccine for H1N1, they are unlikely to be able to respond quickly enough. Firms can produce perhaps a billion doses of seasonal vaccine every year. The details of dosing for a pandemic vaccine are not yet known, but it is clear that even if all the capacity was switched to pandemic flu there would still be a huge global shortfall. Keiji Fukuda of the WHO summed it up this way: "There's much greater vaccine capacity than there was a few years ago, but there is not enough vaccine capacity to instantly make vaccines for the entire world's population for influenza."

Switching production also poses risks. A lack of vaccines for seasonal flu guarantees that many unprotected people will die of the otherwise mundane version of influenza. Nor is there any guarantee that, having switched production, a second wave of an H1N1 strain will indeed be deadly. So producing pandemic vaccines as a precaution may turn out to be a waste of resources with deadly results. Or it may save millions of lives. No one knows.

The main problem is that egg-based manufacturing cannot mount a rapid response. It could take only a few more weeks for the WHO and CDC to develop a "seed" strain of the pandemic virus, but experts say producers would then need four to six months before they could create large volumes of vaccine.

Could more innovative manufacturing techniques help? One promising approach involves growing vaccines not in eggs but in cell cultures, which is speedy and easily scaled up. Another is to add adjuvants, which are catalysts that improve the efficacy of a vaccine and reduce the amount of active ingredient required.

A number of companies have been hoping to get such technologies to the market by 2011 or 2012, and some might be able to help with any shortfall should there be a pandemic later this year. Anthony Fauci, head of America's National Institute of Allergy and Infectious Diseases, says the American government has been funding many such firms in preparation for bioterrorism and pandemics. But he points out that none of the firms has so far got a pandemic flu vaccine past safety trials. "They are not ready for prime-time," he says.

Yet desperate times may lead to desperate measures. Cell-based manufacturing is already used to make vaccines against many other diseases, so it might win rapid approval for flu. European regulators have been more enthusiastic than American ones about allowing adjuvants in flu vaccines. Mexican officials are reportedly in discussions with biotech firms to build flexible vaccine-facilities quickly. The WHO this week called such novel approaches a risky "leap of faith". But if a crisis does engulf the world, that may be a leap some are willing to make.

9

Vaccines Prevent Infectious Diseases

National Institute of Allergy and Infectious Diseases

A part of the National Institutes of Health, the National Institute of Allergy and Infectious Diseases (NIAID) is a federal research agency that conducts basic and applied research to better understand, treat, and ultimately prevent infectious, immunologic, and allergic diseases.

With the arrival of vaccines, numerous infectious diseases that struck hundreds of thousands of people in the United States each year—oftentimes lethally—have been eradicated and nearly forgotten today. Vaccines are effective because they artificially create acquired immunity, which naturally occurs after a person is infected and survives. This is achieved through delivering either a partial or weakened microbe to simulate infection that does not cause illness. Vaccines protect the immunized and the people around them; when a critical number of members in a community is vaccinated against a particular disease, known as herd immunity, the group is much less likely to get the disease. In addition, routine childhood immunization has greatly reduced the economic costs of infectious diseases.

Chances are you never had diphtheria. You probably don't know anyone who has suffered from this disease, either. In fact, you may not know what diphtheria is. Similarly, dis-

National Institute of Allergy and Infectious Diseases, "Vaccines: Understanding," www.niaid.nih.gov. http://www.niaid.nih.gov/topics/vaccines/understanding/Pages /whatVaccine.aspx. http://www.niaid.nih.gov/topics/vaccines/understanding/Pages /vaccineBenefits.aspx. http://www.niaid.nih.gov/topics/vaccines/understanding/Pages /howWork.aspx. Courtesy: National Institute of Allergy and Infectious Diseases.

eases like whooping cough (pertussis), measles, mumps, and German measles (rubella) may be unfamiliar to you. In the 19th and early 20th centuries, these illnesses struck hundreds of thousands of people in the United States each year, mostly children, and tens of thousands of people died. The names of these diseases were frightening household words. Today, they are all but forgotten. That change happened largely because of vaccines.

Chances are you've been vaccinated against diphtheria. You may even have been exposed to the bacterium that causes it, but the vaccine prepared your body to fight off the disease so quickly that you were unaware of the infection. Vaccines take advantage of your body's natural ability to learn how to combat many disease-causing germs, or microbes, that attack it. What's more, your body "remembers" how to protect itself from the microbes it has encountered before. Collectively, the parts of your body that remember and repel microbes are called the immune system. Without the immune system, the simplest illness—even the common cold—could quickly turn deadly.

Vaccines can prevent a disease from occurring in the first place, rather than attempt to cure it after the fact.

On average, your immune system takes more than a week to learn how to fight off an unfamiliar microbe. Sometimes that isn't soon enough. Stronger microbes can spread through your body faster than the immune system can fend them off. Your body often gains the upper hand after a few weeks, but in the meantime you are sick. Certain microbes are so powerful, or virulent, that they can overwhelm or escape your body's natural defenses. In those situations, vaccines can make all the difference.

Traditional vaccines contain either parts of microbes or whole microbes that have been killed or weakened so that they don't cause disease. When your immune system confronts these harmless versions of the germs, it quickly clears them from your body. In other words, vaccines trick your immune system to teach your body important lessons about how to defeat its opponents.

Vaccine Benefits

Once your immune system is trained to resist a disease, you are said to be immune to it. Before vaccines, the only way to become immune to a disease was to actually get it and, with luck, survive it. This is called naturally acquired immunity. With naturally acquired immunity, you suffer the symptoms of the disease and also risk the complications, which can be quite serious or even deadly. In addition, during certain stages of the illness, you may be contagious and pass the disease to family members, friends, or others who come into contact with you.

Vaccines, which provide artificially acquired immunity, are an easier and less risky way to become immune. Vaccines can prevent a disease from occurring in the first place, rather than attempt to cure it after the fact.

Benefits for You and Others

It is also much cheaper to prevent a disease than to treat it. In a 2005 study on the economic impact of routine childhood immunization in the United States, researchers estimated that for every dollar spent, the vaccination program saved more than $5 in direct costs and approximately $11 in additional costs to society.

Vaccines protect not only yourself but also others around you. If your vaccine-primed immune system stops an illness before it starts, you will be contagious for a much shorter period of time, or perhaps not at all. Similarly, when other people are vaccinated, they are less likely to give the disease to you. Vaccines protect not only individuals but entire communities. That is why vaccines are vital to the public health goal of preventing diseases.

If a critical number of people within a community are vaccinated against a particular illness, the entire group becomes less likely to get the disease. This protection is called community, or herd, immunity. On the other hand, if too many people in a community do not get vaccinations, diseases can reappear. In 1989, low vaccination rates allowed a measles outbreak to occur in the United States. The outbreak resulted in more than 55,000 cases of measles and 136 measles-associated deaths.

How Vaccines Work

The human immune system is a complex network of cells and organs that evolved to fight off infectious microbes. Much of the immune system's work is carried out by an army of various specialized cells, each type designed to fight disease in a particular way. The invading microbes first run into the vanguard of this army, which includes white blood cells called macrophages (literally, "big eaters"). The macrophages engulf as many of the microbes as they can.

Every microbe carries its own unique set of antigens, which are central to creating vaccines.

Antigens Sound the Alarm

How do the macrophages recognize the microbes? All cells and microbes wear a "uniform" made up of molecules that cover their surfaces. Each human cell displays unique marker molecules unique to you. Microbes display different marker molecules unique to them. The macrophages and other cells of your immune system use these markers to distinguish among the cells that are part of your body, harmless bacteria that reside in your body, and harmful invading microbes that need to be destroyed.

The molecules on a microbe that identify it as foreign and stimulate the immune system to attack it are called "antigens." Every microbe carries its own unique set of antigens, which are central to creating vaccines.

Macrophages digest most parts of the microbes but save the antigens and carry them back to the lymph nodes, bean-sized organs scattered throughout your body where immune system cells congregate. In these nodes, macrophages sound the alarm by "regurgitating" the antigens, displaying them on their surfaces so other cells, such as specialized defensive white blood cells called lymphocytes, can recognize them.

Lymphocytes Take Over

There are two major kinds of lymphocytes, T cells and B cells, and they do their own jobs in fighting off infection. T cells function either offensively or defensively. The offensive T cells don't attack the microbe directly, but they use chemical weapons to eliminate the human cells that have already been infected. Because they have been "programmed" by their exposure to the microbe's antigen, these cytotoxic T cells, also called killer T cells, can "sense" diseased cells that are harboring the microbe. The killer T cells latch onto these cells and release chemicals that destroy the infected cells and the microbes inside.

The defensive T cells, also called helper T cells, defend the body by secreting chemical signals that direct the activity of other immune system cells. Helper T cells assist in activating killer T cells, and helper T cells also stimulate and work closely with B cells. The work done by T cells is called the cellular or cell-mediated immune response.

B cells make and secrete extremely important molecular weapons called antibodies. Antibodies usually work by first grabbing onto the microbe's antigen, and then sticking to and coating the microbe. Antibodies and antigens fit together like pieces of a jigsaw puzzle—if their shapes are compatible, they bind to each other.

Each antibody can usually fit with only one antigen. The immune system keeps a supply of millions and possibly billions of different antibodies on hand to be prepared for any foreign invader. It does this by constantly creating millions of new B cells. About 50 million B cells circulate in each teaspoonful of human blood, and almost every B cell—through random genetic shuffling—produces a unique antibody that it displays on its surface.

When these B cells come into contact with their matching microbial antigen, they are stimulated to divide into many larger cells, called plasma cells, which secrete mass quantities of antibodies to bind to the microbe.

Antibodies in Action

The antibodies secreted by B cells circulate throughout the human body and attack the microbes that have not yet infected any cells but are lurking in the blood or the spaces between cells. When antibodies gather on the surface of a microbe, it becomes unable to function. Antibodies signal macrophages and other defensive cells to come eat the microbe. Antibodies also work with other defensive molecules that circulate in the blood, called complement proteins, to destroy microbes.

The work of B cells is called the humoral immune response, or simply the antibody response. The goal of most vaccines is to stimulate this response. In fact, many infectious microbes can be defeated by antibodies alone, without any help from killer T cells.

Clearing the Infection: Memory Cells and Natural Immunity

When T cells and antibodies begin to eliminate the microbe faster than it can reproduce, the immune system finally has the upper hand. Gradually, the virus disappears from the body.

Vaccines teach the immune system by mimicking a natural infection.

After the body eliminates the disease, some microbe-fighting B cells and T cells are converted into memory cells. Memory B cells can quickly divide into plasma cells and make more antibody if needed. Memory T cells can divide and grow into a microbe-fighting army. If re-exposure to the infectious microbe occurs, the immune system will quickly recognize how to stop the infection.

How Vaccines Mimic Infection

Vaccines teach the immune system by mimicking a natural infection. For example, the yellow fever vaccine, first widely used in 1938, contains a weakened form of the virus that doesn't cause disease or reproduce very well. Human macrophages can't tell that the vaccine viruses are weakened, so they engulf the viruses as if they were dangerous. In the lymph nodes, the macrophages present yellow fever antigen to T cells and B cells.

A response from yellow-fever-specific T cells is activated. B cells secrete yellow fever antibodies. The weakened viruses in the vaccine are quicky eliminated. The mock infection is cleared, and humans are left with a supply of memory T and B cells for future protection against yellow fever.

10

Vaccine Exemptions Must Be Protected

Joseph Mercola

Joseph Mercola is a physician and author of numerous books on health and the human diet.

Vaccine exemptions based on religious or personal beliefs are routinely blamed for recent outbreaks of infectious diseases, leaving many Americans fighting for their right to opt out of involuntarily immunization. However, research and statistics demonstrate these outbreaks have occurred mostly among vaccinated people. Contrary to common misperception, immunity gained through vaccination is significantly different and inferior to naturally acquired immunity from exposure to infection, but pro-vaccine advocates maintain that vaccines offer the same protection. And immunizations have the potential to trigger responses that result in longterm illness and disability. Whatever their vaccine choices, Americans need to be accurately informed about the risks and legal options to refuse immunizations for themselves and their families.

The featured article in the latest newsletter from Children's Hospital of Philadelphia (CHOP) gets straight to the point with its headline. *Back to School—Is the Child Sitting Next to Yours Immunized?*

The article goes on to berate vaccine exemption options and parents who use personal belief exemptions to opt-out of vaccines for their children. It stops short of ordering parents to march into their children's classrooms and demand to know who's vaccinated and who's not (health privacy laws prevent that anyway).

It peppers you with enough scare tactics—along with links to information on vaccine exemptions and states that allow personal belief exemptions—to leave readers convinced they need to do something to stop vaccine exemptions.

All across the United States, people are fighting for their right to choose not to be injected with vaccines against their will, and this is just the latest tactic in a coordinated effort aimed at eliminating all vaccine exemptions.

The Gates Foundation is even funding surveillance of anti-vaccine groups. Seth C. Kalichman, professor at the Department of Psychology, University of Connecticut recently received a $100,000 grant to establish an Anti-Vaccine Surveillance and Alert System.

The intention is to "establish an internet-based global monitoring and rapid alert system for finding, analyzing, and counteracting misinformation communication campaigns regarding vaccines to support global immunization efforts," GreenMedInfo.com reports.

My strong guess is that some of the best sources for truthful information like NVIC.org and this web site have already been targeted by the Gates Foundation.

In light of that, it's not surprising that vaccine groups are trying to turn citizens against each other in an effort to squelch opposition and free will on this matter. According to CHOP:

". . . these decisions, often referred to as personal belief exemptions, have been traced to recent cases of pertussis, measles and mumps in several states. Currently, 20 states allow personal belief exemptions.

Many people do not realize that these choices put not only their own children at risk, but also those around them because the more people in a community who are immune to a disease, the lower the chance that the disease will spread throughout the community. This is called herd immunity. So, even those who may not be immune will have a decreased chance of getting the disease."

Published studies into the outbreaks have revealed that a lot of the blame should be placed on ineffective vaccines—not on the unvaccinated minority.

First of all, there are only 18 states—not 20—that allow personal belief, philosophical or conscientious belief exemptions to vaccination, in addition to 48 states that allow religious belief exemptions. . . .

Unvaccinated Population Falsely Blamed for Ineffective Vaccines

Recent disease outbreaks were traced back to personal belief exemptions. . . . Really?

That's just not reality, and if you take the time to look into the truthfulness of that statement, you'll see it simply does not hold up. Many outbreaks of pertussis (whooping cough), measles, and mumps have *occurred primarily in people who were vaccinated*, and no one seems to be able to fully explain how that is the fault of those who are unvaccinated. . . .

If the vaccine theory was correct, these people should have been protected because they were vaccinated. Published studies into the outbreaks have revealed that a lot of the blame should be placed on *ineffective vaccines*—not on the unvaccinated minority.

Consider the following findings about the last two whooping cough (pertussis) outbreaks.

In 2010, the largest outbreak of whooping cough in over 50 years occurred in California. Around that same time, a scare campaign was launched in California by Pharma-funded medical trade associations, state health officials and national media, targeting people opting out of receiving pertussis vaccine, falsely accusing them of causing the outbreak.

However, research published in March of this year [2012] shows that 81 percent of 2010 California whooping cough cases in people under the age of 18 occurred in those who were fully up to date on the whooping cough vaccine. Eleven percent had received at least one shot, but not the entire recommended series, and *only eight percent of those stricken were unvaccinated.* . . .

B. pertussis whooping cough is a cyclical disease with natural increases that tend to occur every 4–5 years, no matter how high the vaccination rate is in a population using DPT/DTaP or Tdap [diptheria, pertussis, and tetanus] vaccines on a widespread basis. Whole cell DPT vaccines used in the U.S. from the 1950's until the late 1990's were estimated to be 63 to 94 percent effective and studies showed that vaccine-acquired immunity fell to about 40 percent after seven years.

In the study cited above, the researchers noted the vaccine's effectiveness was only 41 percent among 2- to 7-year-olds and a dismal 24 percent among those aged 8–12. With this shockingly low rate of DTaP vaccine effectiveness, the questionable solution public health officials have come up with is to declare that everybody has to get *three* primary shots and *three follow-up booster shots* in order to get long-lasting protection—and that's provided the vaccine gives you any protection at all!

The Washington State Secretary of Health also declared a pertussis epidemic on April 3, 2012, in response to a 1,300 percent increase in pertussis cases compared to 2011. Scientists are now considering adding a *seventh* inoculation, in order to boost protection against whooping cough.

According to a recent article and video by KPBS:

"New research confirms the whooping cough vaccine is failing at a higher rate than expected, and scientists are considering

adding a seventh dose to the national immunization schedule published by the Centers for Disease Control and Prevention. Two recent studies have found the majority of people getting sick are up to date with their immunizations."

This vaccine is supposed to improve immunity to measles, mumps and rubella . . . yet 77 percent of the 1,000+ who came down with mumps were vaccinated.

Mumps and Measles Vaccines Are Also Failing

- *Mumps:* In 2010, more than 1,000 people in New Jersey and New York were also sickened with mumps. In the US, children typically receive their mumps vaccination as part of the measles, mumps, and rubella (MMR) vaccine. The U.S. Centers for Disease Control and Prevention (CDC) advises children to receive their first dose between 12 and 18 months, and their second between the ages of 4 and 6.

  This vaccine is supposed to improve immunity to measles, mumps and rubella . . . yet 77 percent of the 1,000+ who came down with mumps were vaccinated. Similarly, in 2006, when mumps infected more than 6,500 people in the United States, cases occurred primarily among college students who had received two doses of MMR vaccine. At that time, just about the only people who were truly immune to mumps were older Americans who had recovered from mumps as children, and therefore had received natural, lifelong immunity.

- *Measles:* The 1989 measles epidemic in the region of Quebec was largely attributed to incomplete vaccination coverage—until a study into the outbreak disclosed that the outbreak occurred in a population that had *99 percent* vaccination coverage. The researchers concluded that: "*Incomplete vaccination coverage is not a valid explanation for the Quebec City measles outbreak.*"

Conflicts of Interest— Not Science—Influence Most Vaccine Recommendations

The CHOP newsletter is delivered by email periodically to anyone who signs up for it, and almost always contains advice on getting all children vaccinated. The Vaccine Education Center at CHOP says it's funded by endowed chairs and "does not receive support from pharmaceutical companies."

But it neglects to mention that the hospital indirectly benefits from drug company money that helps fund endowed chairs like Merck's Maurice R. Hilleman Professor of Vaccinology, which is currently held by Paul Offit, who not only is very public about his belief that infants could theoretically safely handle 10,000 vaccines all at once; he also openly opposes personal belief vaccine exemptions. Rarely is it mentioned that Offit has a financial stake in the vaccine industry, as he invented one of the vaccines CHOP promotes. He's also served on the scientific advisory board of Merck.

Offit's personal beliefs about forcing people to involuntarily use vaccines, which violates the informed consent ethic in medicine, along with the inaccurate statements he makes about vaccine safety, which are not backed by solid scientific evidence, are echoed throughout CHOP's pro-forced vaccination propaganda. For example, one of their Q&A brochures answers the question: *Can too many vaccines overwhelm an infant's immune system?* with the following statement:

"*No. Compared to the immunological challenges that infants handle every day, the challenge from the immunological compo-*

nents in vaccines is minuscule. Babies begin dealing with immunological challenges at birth. The mother's womb is a sterile environment, free from viruses, bacteria, parasites and fungi. But after babies pass through the birth canal and enter the world, they are immediately colonized with trillions of bacteria, which means that they carry the bacteria on their bodies but aren't infected by them. These bacteria live on the skin, nose, throat and intestines. To make sure that colonizing bacteria don't invade the bloodstream and cause harm, babies constantly make antibodies against them.

. . .Given that infants are colonized with trillions of bacteria, that each bacterium contains between 2,000 and 6,000 immunological components and that infants are infected with numerous viruses, the challenge from the 150 immunological components in vaccines is minuscule compared to what infants manage every day."

This is an astounding comparison and shockingly ignorant of foundational physiology.

Not only do these ignorant statements dismiss and disparage the role of beneficial gut bacteria—which we now know are absolutely essential and vital for human health and well-being—and characterize normal gut bacteria as potentially harmful, but there is a false characterization of the immunological challenge posed by multiple vaccines, each of which can contain either live or killed viruses and a number of different adjuvants and chemicals, injected into the tiny body of an infant. . . .

The Difference Between Natural and Vaccine-Induced Immunity

Many still believe vaccines provide identical immunity to that obtained when you are naturally exposed to an infection. This widespread misconception needs to be corrected.

The presumed result of a vaccination is to help you build immunity to potentially harmful organisms that cause disease.

What many fail to appreciate is that your body's immune system is already designed to do this in response to naturally occurring infectious agents that you are constantly exposed to throughout life. One major difference between vaccine-induced immunity and natural immunity stems from *how* you're exposed to these organisms.

Most organisms that cause infection enter your body through the mucous membranes of your nose, mouth, lungs or your digestive tract.

Your immune system simply was not designed to be injected with lab-altered disease-causing organisms.

These mucous membranes have their own immune system, called the secretory IgA immune system. It is a different system from the one activated when a vaccine is injected into your body. Your IgA immune system is your body's first line of defense and its job is to address the infectious microorganism at their entry points, thus reducing or even eliminating the need for activation of your body's entire immune system.

However, when a laboratory altered or created infectious microorganism is injected into your body with a vaccine and, especially when combined with an immune adjuvant, such as aluminum, your IgA immune system is bypassed, stimulating your immune system to mount a very strong inflammatory response.

Vaccines can also trigger such a strong inflammatory response that the inflammation becomes chronic and leads to chronic illness or disability. (People with a personal or family history of severe allergy or autoimmunity should be cautious about vaccination because they already have a genetic predisposition to inflammatory responses that do not resolve and can lead to chronic health problems.)

Injecting these lab-altered microorganisms into your body in an attempt to provoke an atypical, temporary immunity is clearly not the same way your body develops naturally-acquired immunity. Your immune system simply was not designed to be injected with lab-altered disease-causing organisms in this manner. While I am a great fan and advocate of technology it is very clear to me that this is one reason why vaccines almost always only provide a much more temporary immunity compared to naturally acquired immunity.

Additionally, this plays a large role in why vaccines have the potential to do serious damage to your health.

Since vaccines bypass your natural first-line defense (your IgA immune system), they are clearly inferior to natural immunity and fail to provide the same kind of long lasting protection from future disease as they provide *typically inferior immunity* compared to that your body would acquire by experiencing and healing from the natural disease. In the case of mumps, for instance, immunity is typically permanent for those who contract the disease during childhood.

What You Need to Know About "Herd Immunity"

The National Institute of Allergy and Infectious Diseases describes vaccine-induced herd immunity, also labeled "community immunity" by public health doctors as follows:

"When a critical portion of a community is immunized against a contagious disease, most members of the community are protected against that disease because there is little opportunity for an outbreak. Even those who are not eligible for certain vaccines—such as infants, pregnant women, or immunocompromised individuals—get some protection because the spread of contagious disease is contained. This is known as 'community immunity.'"

The problem is that there is in fact such a thing as *natural herd immunity*. But what they've done is they've taken this natural phenomenon and assumed that vaccines will work the same way. However, vaccines do not confer the same kind of immunity as experiencing the natural disease, and the science clearly shows that there's a big difference between naturally acquired herd immunity and vaccine-induced herd immunity. . . .

There is a basic human right . . . to refuse to allow substances you consider to be harmful, toxic or poisonous to be forced upon you.

Vaccines are designed to *trick* your body's immune system into producing protective antibodies needed to resist any future infection. However, your body is smarter than that. The artificial stimulation of your immune system produced by lab-altered bacteria and viruses simply does not replicate the exact response that your immune system mounts when naturally encountering the infectious microorganism. . . .

Why We Must Defend Vaccine Exemptions

All Americans need to know their options for legally opting-out of vaccinations, and you also need to know *why* it's so important to protect this legal option, whether you choose to use every federally recommended vaccine for yourself and your children or not.

No matter what vaccination choices you make for yourself or your family, there is a basic human right to be fully informed about all risks and have the ability to refuse to allow substances you consider to be harmful, toxic or poisonous to be forced upon you.

Unfortunately, the partnership between government health agencies and vaccine manufacturers is getting closer and closer. There is some serious discrimination against Americans, who want to be free to exercise their human right to informed consent to medical risk-taking when it comes to making voluntary decisions about which vaccines they and their children use. We cannot allow that happen!

11

Travelers Risk Contracting and Spreading Infectious Diseases

Stephen M. Ostroff

Stephen M. Ostroff is the acting physician general for the Pennsylvania Department of Health.

The accelerated pace and frequency of human travel have given infectious diseases opportunities to spread more rapidly and wider than before. In 2009, the pandemic of influenza virus H1N1 was traced to visitors of Mexico, making its way to dozens of nations within less than two months. Severe acute respiratory syndrome (SARS)—which became a global epidemic in 2003— was attributed to a traveling Chinese professor who infected others in his hotel. Vaccine-preventable disease has been reintroduced by travelers and adoptees into regions where it has disappeared. Furthermore, vectorborne illnesses transmitted by travelers have caused outbreaks of pathogens once restricted to geographical areas, and large gatherings of people—characterized by close contact and intermingling—have caused the spread of disease.

Since humans began moving from one place to another, they have offered free passage to pathogens, on themselves or in their belongings, and the consequences of such microbial hitchhiking have, at times, altered the course of history.

Stephen M. Ostroff, "Chapter 1: Perspectives: The Role of the Traveler in Translocation of Disease," *2012 Yellow Book*, edited by Centers for Disease Control and Prevention, Atlanta, GA: Centers for Disease Control and Prevention, 2012. http://wwwnc.cdc.gov /travel/yellowbook/2012/chapter-1-introduction/perspectives-the-role-of-the-traveler-in -translocation-of-disease.htm.

Among the more notable examples are the great plagues that swept into Europe from Asia during the Middle Ages, the importation of smallpox to the Americas by European explorers, and the reverse movement of syphilis into Europe in those same returning explorers.

Although the movement of pathogens through travel is not a new phenomenon, today's increasing pace and scale of global human movement have enhanced the opportunities for disease spread. HIV infection, with symptoms that may be delayed for years, spread around the world less than a decade after it was recognized. In the twenty-first century, no place on the globe is more than a day from any other location, which gives even diseases with short incubation periods unprecedented opportunities for rapid spread. The following examples from the last decade illustrate the role travel plays in the translocation of infectious diseases. They also remind us that all travelers should take steps to prevent bringing more than luggage to their destination.

Influenza

Two new forms of influenza have recently emerged. One is avian influenza A (H5N1), which was first observed during a limited-scale outbreak in Hong Kong in 1997. It reappeared in Vietnam in 2003 and has been in continuous circulation ever since. Even though H5N1 has primarily affected poultry, from 2003 through 2009, 458 human illnesses in 15 countries were reported, with an alarming case-fatality ratio of 62%. The countries with the most human disease (Indonesia, Vietnam, and Egypt) are tourist destinations, but no international travelers have become ill, largely because close contact with infected poultry is the primary risk factor for infection, and no sustained human-to-human transmission has been observed. However, movement of the virus between countries in goods carried by conveyances and animals has been documented.

In contrast, the rapid spread of 2009 pandemic influenza A (H1N1) was aided by infected travelers, both those who were symptomatic and those who were in the incubation stage. Although the virus was first identified in southern California in April 2009, human illnesses appeared weeks earlier in Mexico. Infected travelers who had visited Mexico were quickly detected in other parts of the world. An analysis of air traffic patterns found a very strong correlation between the volume of air travel from Mexico to a country and the likelihood H1N1 was identified in that location during the early stages of the pandemic. Aided by travel, this new virus found its way to dozens of countries in less than 2 months after it was identified, resulting in a June 2009 pandemic designation by the World Health Organization. The H1N1 pandemic vividly demonstrates the potential for global dissemination of pathogens in a highly interconnected world.

SARS

The severe acute respiratory syndrome (SARS) epidemic of 2003 is another major example of the role of travel in the spread of infectious diseases in the twenty-first century. In February 2003, a professor from southern China, who was caring for patients with an unrecognized respiratory illness, traveled to a family wedding in Hong Kong while he was ill. His infection spread to 10 other travelers in his hotel, who then boarded airplanes to other parts of Asia, North America, and Europe, setting off a global epidemic of SARS that resulted in 8,098 cases and 774 deaths in 29 countries. Fortunately, characteristics of the virus, transmission dynamics of the disease, and aggressive public health measures contained the virus within months, but not before SARS produced widespread fear, and economic and political turmoil. SARS had a major influence on the revisions to the International Health Regulations in 2005.

Childhood Vaccine-Preventable Diseases

Vaccination programs have substantially reduced the global prevalence of childhood infectious diseases. In the Western Hemisphere, measles transmission has been effectively eliminated, and diseases like mumps and rubella are at historical lows. Globally, poliomyelitis has been targeted for eradication, and by the early 2000s, transmission of indigenous poliovirus was confined to only 4 countries. However, these diseases are all highly transmissible and can easily spread in infected travelers; endemic transmission has been reestablished in some previously polio-free areas.

Several recent large outbreaks of mumps in the United States are directly traceable to travel-related importation from Great Britain.

Measles

In the United States, all recent clusters of measles have been associated with travel. These episodes have been precipitated by visitors from areas of the world where measles continues to circulate due to low vaccination coverage, susceptible US travelers going abroad, and overseas adoptees. These importations then ignite outbreaks because of waning population immunity, which is fueled largely by parents who elect not to vaccinate their children. During the first half of 2008, 13% of measles cases with an identified source were imported, and 76% of the remaining cases were the result of subsequent local transmission. In the previous decade, 20%–60% of cases were imported, and subsequent spread was much more limited.

Mumps

Several recent large outbreaks of mumps in the United States are directly traceable to travel-related importation from Great

Britain. A 2006 outbreak centered in Iowa, likely fueled by spring break travel, resulted in more than 2,500 cases across 11 states. A more recent outbreak that began in mid-2009, resulting in more than 2,000 cases in New York City and surrounding states, largely centered around an Orthodox Jewish community. This outbreak was started by a single traveler to Great Britain who returned to a summer camp in New York State. Mumps then spread to campers and staff, who carried it home to New York City and ignited sustained transmission for many months.

Polio

In 2002, only 6 countries had circulating indigenous wild-type poliovirus, but from 2002 through 2007, wild-type poliovirus spread to 27 previously disease-free countries in Africa and Asia through the movement of infected travelers. Northern Nigeria was the source of most of these illnesses, which reached all the way to Indonesia. Vaccination campaigns, guided by laboratory-based surveillance, largely disrupted transmission in these places, but travel continues to result in the spread of polio. In 2008–2009, there were 47 introductions or reintroductions of the virus into 17 African countries, all originating from Nigeria or India, resulting in 255 subsequent cases. In 2010, even as polio incidence decreased in Nigeria and India, 2 large outbreaks demonstrated the risk of introduction from poliovirus reservoirs. Spread of poliovirus into Tajikistan from India caused an outbreak of 458 cases and, subsequently, 18 cases in 2 other Central Asian republics and Russia. In the Republic of the Congo, a large outbreak (more than 300 suspected cases as of late November 2010) resulted after introduction from Angola, posing further risk of spread elsewhere. Although these cases do not threaten most travelers, polio remains a serious concern for migrants, pilgrims, and people displaced by conflict; outbreaks heavily tax the public health resources of affected countries.

Vectorborne Infections

Several mosquito-transmitted diseases have expanded their range in the last decade. West Nile virus was introduced into New York City in 1999 and, in the next several years, spread throughout the Western Hemisphere, resulting in millions of human infections. The source and mode of introduction are unknown; an infected traveler is a distinct possibility, although importation of infected birds or mosquitoes is considered more likely.

For 2 other major vectorborne infections (dengue and chikungunya), the role of travelers is much clearer. Neither of these viruses has an avian intermediary, and humans are amplifying hosts for both viruses, effectively moving these viruses from place to place. Dengue outbreaks are expanding in scale and scope, especially in Asia and South America. Twice since 2000, the virus has made incursions into the United States via infected travelers. In 2001, local transmission was detected on Maui in Hawaii for the first time since the 1940s, resulting in 122 cases. The source was travelers from French Polynesia, which was experiencing an outbreak at the time. In 2009–2010, local dengue transmission was seen in the Florida Keys, also for the first time in decades. More than 70 cases were identified, including in tourists to the Florida Keys from other areas of the United States. The source of introduction is unknown, although many people from areas where dengue is endemic transit through the area.

[Numerous] examples highlight the diversity of opportunities for microbial movement afforded by travel. No amount of vigilance is likely to eliminate such opportunities, especially since microbes can be silent travelers.

Chikungunya virus was largely restricted to Africa and Asia until it began to appear in islands of the Indian Ocean in 2005, after an outbreak in Kenya in 2004. From there, it crossed to the Indian subcontinent in 2006, touching off major disease outbreaks, especially in southern India. Sizeable numbers of travelers to Indian Ocean tourist destinations and India have returned to Europe, North America, and Australia infected with chikungunya virus, and infected Indian nationals have also been seen in these locations. Chikungunya virus can be introduced into these areas in the same way that West Nile virus was introduced into the United States in 1999. Such events have taken place in several areas, including northern Italy in 2007, and southeast France and south-central China in 2010. The source for translocation in Italy was a viremic traveler from India. A total of 205 locally acquired cases were acquired through infected *Aedes albopictus* mosquitoes, an invasive species which appeared in the area in the early 1990s. In contrast to West Nile in North America, chikungunya virus does not appear to have persisted in northern Italy. Many countries that have a viable vector for chikungunya virus remain at risk for importation and local transmission.

Disease Associated with Global Gatherings

The pilgrimage to Mecca is the world's largest annual event, drawing approximately 2 million Muslims from across the globe to Saudi Arabia. The history of the Hajj pilgrimage serves as an example of how diseases can spread during a global mass gathering, and can spread to home countries of returning travelers. The intermingling and close contact offer ample opportunities for transmission of infectious diseases and rapid dissemination as pilgrims return home. In 2000, this occurred with *Neisseria meningitidis* serogroup W-135, despite requirements for pilgrims to be vaccinated against meningococcal disease. Some vaccines used at that time did not cover this serogroup. After the event, 90 infections in returnees and their contacts were seen across Europe. In contrast, the number of infections in North America, where quadrivalent vaccine that covered W-135 was in use, was small.

The outbreak strain of W-135 also quickly surfaced across areas of Africa, Asia, the Middle East, and the Indian Ocean, altering the epidemiologic patterns of meningococcal disease. As a result of this outbreak and similar cases in 2001, pilgrims to the Hajj are now required to be vaccinated with the quadrivalent vaccine.

These examples highlight the diversity of opportunities for microbial movement afforded by travel. No amount of vigilance is likely to eliminate such opportunities, especially since microbes can be silent travelers. However, all travelers should take precautions to prevent the spread of disease.

Organizations to Contact

The editors have compiled the following list of organizations concerned with the issues debated in this book. The descriptions are derived from materials provided by the organizations. All have publications or information available for interested readers. The list was compiled on the date of publication of the present volume; the information provided here may change. Be aware that many organizations take several weeks or longer to respond to inquiries, so allow as much time as possible.

The Carter Center
One Copenhill, 453 Freedom Parkway, Atlanta, GA   30307
(404) 420-5100
e-mail: carterweb@emory.edu
website: www.cartercenter.org

Founded by former president and First Lady Jimmy and Rosalynn Carter, The Carter Center is a nonprofit organization dedicated to "creating a world in which every man, woman, and child has the opportunity to enjoy good health and live in peace." The website includes information regarding the Center's work in preventing disease in Latin America and Africa. The site also provides videos, brochures, and articles.

Center for Infectious Disease Research and Policy (CIDRAP)
University of Minnesota, Academic Health Center
420 Delaware St. SE, MMC 263, Minneapolis, MN   55455
(612) 626-6770
e-mail: cidrap@umn.edu
website: www.cidrap.umn.edu

CIDRAP, located at the University of Minnesota, addresses public health preparedness and emerging infectious disease response. Some of their main work focuses on pandemic influenza preparedness, bioterrorism response, and information gathering and dissemination. The website offers sections on influenza, bioterrorism, biosecurity, food safety, and other topics such as severe acute respiratory syndrome (SARS), West Nile virus, and monkeypox, complete with many articles, facts, and resources.

Centers for Disease Control and Prevention (CDC)

1600 Clifton Rd., Atlanta, GA   30333
(800) 232-4636
e-mail: cdcinfo@cdc.gov
website: www.cdc.gov

A division of the US Department of Health and Human Services, the CDC is the nation's premier public health organization. The mission of the CDC is "to promote health and quality of life by preventing and controlling disease, injury, and disability." Its website provides a wealth of useful and understandable materials on the subject of infectious diseases, including fact sheets, publications, news articles, and statistics.

Committee to Reduce Infection Deaths (RID)

Attn. Betsy McCaughey, 185 East 85th St., Suite 35B
New York, NY   10028
(212) 369-3329
e-mail: betsy@hospitalinfection.org
website: www.hospitalinfection.org

RID is a nonprofit educational campaign and advocacy group devoted to fighting the causes of hospital infections. Their website includes information about methicillin-resistant *Staphylococcus aureus* (MRSA), the state of hygiene in American hospitals, and a list of fifteen steps patients can take to reduce their risk for hospital-originated infections. Also listed on the site are links to other publications, a newsletter, and blog. Educational materials can be ordered through the website.

Flu.gov

US Department of Health and Human Services (HHS)
200 Independence Ave. SW, Washington, DC   20201

(877) 696-6775
website: www.pandemicflu.gov

HHS offers a large, up-to-date website that provides one-stop access to all US government information regarding influenza. It includes sections on health and safety, global issues, articles on the economic impact of flu, a newsroom, and glossary, serving students and others interested in flu and the likelihood of a future pandemic.

Global Solutions for Infectious Diseases (GSID)
830 Dubuque Ave., South San Francisco, CA 94080
(650) 228-7900 • fax: (650) 228-7901
website: www.gsid.org

GSID is a nonprofit organization dedicated to the expansion of low-cost diagnostic tools and prevention of infectious diseases in less developed countries. The group is targeting HIV/AIDS and is working to develop a vaccine for the diseases. The GSID website has many articles as well as descriptions of its worldwide projects.

Infectious Disease Research Institute (IDRI)
1124 Columbia St., Suite 400, Seattle, WA 98104
(206) 381-0883 • fax: (206) 381-3678
e-mail: office@idri.org
website: www.idri.org

IDRI is a nonprofit biotech research organization whose mission is to "target diseases that largely affect individuals living in economically challenged countries that have difficulty meeting the public health burden of disease." Their goal is to find cures and preventative measures to combat these diseases. IDRI's website includes an informative newsletter as well as specific information on diseases such as tuberculosis, malaria, and leprosy, among others.

Malaria Consortium
Head Office Development House, 56-64 Leonard St.
London EC2A 4LT
    United Kingdom

+44 (0)20 7549 0210
e-mail: info@malariaconsortium.org
website: www.malariaconsortium.org

The Malaria Consortium is an international organization based in the United Kingdom dedicated to improving the prevention and treatment of malaria in Africa and Asia. It maintains most of its offices and programs in these two continents. The group's website offers an extensive collection of fact sheets, case studies, and articles about malaria as well as many links to additional informational resources concerning the disease.

National Foundation for Infectious Diseases (NFID)

4733 Bethesda Ave., Suite 750, Bethesda, MD   20814
(301) 656-0003 • fax: (301) 907-0878
website: www.nfid.org

NFID is a nonprofit organization whose mission is to educate the public and healthcare workers about the causes, treatment, and prevention of infectious diseases. The organization's website includes a media center, fact sheets, and publications, as well as specific information on meningitis, pertussis, tetanus, diphtheria, influenza, pneumococcal bacteria, and shingles.

National Patient Safety Foundation (NPSF)

268 Summer St., 6th Floor, Boston, MA   02210
website: www.npsf.org

NPSF is a nonprofit advocacy group dedicated to improving patient safety. Its website includes significant information on MRSA infections and prevention as well as publications, articles, and links to other sources of information concerning patients and infectious diseases. The foundation also holds events such as its Annual Patient Safety Congress and Patient Safety Awareness Week.

National Vaccine Information Center (NVIC)

407 Church St., Suite H, Vienna, VA   22180

(703) 938-0342
website: www.nvic.org

NVIC is a nonprofit educational organization. According to the NVIC website, the organization is "dedicated to the prevention of vaccine injuries and deaths through public education and to defending the informed consent ethic." It also helps people who believe they or their family members have been injured by vaccines. The organization's website includes many articles, a blog, and links to other news sources providing information about vaccines.

Vaccine and Infectious Disease Organization (VIDO)
University of Saskatchewan, 120 Veterinary Rd.
Saskatoon   SK, S7N 5E3
   Canada
(306) 966-7465 • fax: (306) 966-7478
website: www.vido.org

VIDO is a nonprofit organization owned by the University of Saskatchewan and supported by the governments of Alberta and Saskatchewan as well as the Canadian government. Its work centers on the development and delivery of new vaccines for humans and animals. The VIDO website includes news about its work, publications, and information about careers and training in the field of immunology.

Vaccine Education Center
Children's Hospital of Philadelphia
34th St. and Civic Center Blvd., Philadelphia, PA   19104
(215) 590-1000
website: www.chop.edu/service/vaccine-education-center/home
.html

The Vaccine Education Center of the Children's Hospital of Philadelphia provides complete and reliable information about vaccines. This information includes videos, DVDs, news articles, and publications as well as a schedule of recommended vaccinations. Readers can order additional educational materials through its website, where links to other resources are offered.

World Health Organization (WHO)
Avenue Appia 20, 1211, Geneva 27
   Switzerland
+41 22 791 21 11
e-mail: info@who.int
website: www.who.int

WHO is the directing and coordinating authority for health of the United Nations. As such, the organization is a global force in issues of health and disease. Its website includes multimedia presentations, fact sheets, news articles, publications, brochures, and statistics. For students of infectious disease, the site also offers online books for download and information on ordering materials through the mail.

Bibliography

Books

John Aberth   *Plagues in World History*. Lanham, MD: Rowman & Littlefield, 2011.

Nancy K. Bristow   *American Pandemic: The Lost Worlds of the 1918 Influenza Epidemic*. New York: Oxford University Press, 2012.

Dorothy H. Crawford   *Deadly Companions: How Microbes Shaped Our History*. New York: Oxford University Press, 2009.

Louise Kuo Habakus and Mary Holland, eds.   *Vaccine Epidemic: How Corporate Greed, Biased Science, and Coercive Government Threaten Our Human Rights, Our Health, and Our Children*. New York: Skyhorse Publishing, 2011.

Mark A. Largent   *Vaccine: The Debate in Modern America*. Baltimore, MD: Johns Hopkins University Press, 2012.

Felissa R. Lashley and Jerry D. Durham, eds.   *Emerging Infectious Diseases: Trends and Issues*. New York: Springer Publishing Company, 2010.

Seth Mnookin   *The Panic Virus: A True Story of Medicine, Science, and Fear*. New York: Simon & Schuster, 2011.

Paul A. Offit   *Deadly Choices: How the Anti-Vaccine Movement Threatens Us All*. New York: Basic Books, 2011.

Mark Pendergrast   *Inside the Outbreaks: The Elite Medical Detectives of the Epidemic Intelligence Service.* Boston: Houghton Mifflin Harcourt, 2010.

David Quammen   *Spillover: Animal Infections and the Next Human Pandemic.* London: Bodley Head, 2012.

Sonia Shah   *The Fever: How Malaria Has Ruled Humankind for 500,000 Years.* New York: Sarah Crichton Books/Farrar, Straus, and Giroux, 2010.

Nathan Wolfe   *The Viral Storm: The Dawn of a New Pandemic Age.* New York: Times Books, 2011.

Periodicals and Internet Sources

Dionne M. Aleman   "Predicting the Spread of Pandemics in Urban Environments," *OR/MS Today*, February 2012.

Carrie Arnold   "Modern-Day Typhoid Marys," *Slate*, December 27, 2012. www.slate.com.

Valerie Bauerlein and Betsy McKay   "Where Could the Next Outbreak of Measles Be?," *Wall Street Journal*, March 20, 2012.

Pam Belluck   "Hospitals Could Stop Infections by Tackling Bacteria Patients Bring In, Studies Find," *New York Times*, January 6, 2010.

Daria Donati and Catarina Flyborg   "Pandemic Preparedness: What More Can We Do?," *Biopharm International*, October 2009.

Economist	"The Cost of Swine Flu," July 27, 2009.
Elon Green	"The 10 Greatest Villains of the AIDS Epidemic," *Alternet*, May 24, 2011. www.alternet.org.
Stephen S. Hall	"The 0.5 Pandemic," *New York*, October 12, 2009.
Katherine Harmon	"What Will the Next Influenza Pandemic Look Like?," *Scientific American*, September 19, 2011.
Barbara K. Kennedy	"Slowing the Spread of Drug-Resistant Diseases Is Goal of New Research Area," PennStateScience, June 22, 2011. http://science.psu.edu.
Alex Perry	"Malaria: Epidemic on the Run," *Time*, September 24, 2011.
Alan Phillips	"Vaccine Exemptions: Do They Really Put Others at Risk?," *Natural News*, February 18, 2012. www.natural news.com.
David Quammen	"The Next Pandemic: Why It Will Come from Wildlife," *Yale Environment 360*, October 4, 2012.
Jordan Carlton Schaul	"Is the 'Hype' on Swine Flu for the Birds or People or All of the Above?," Newswatch National Geographic, August 12, 2012. http://newswatch .nationalgeographic.com.

Spiegel   "Resistant Bacteria: Antibiotics Prove
                    Powerless as Super-Germs Spread,"
                    January 27, 2012.

Index

M

N

O

P